WHITE HOUSE, INC.
WASHINGTON

WHITE HOUSE INC.
EMPLOYEE
HANDBOOK

WHITE HOUSE, INC.

WASHINGTON

WHITE HOUSE INC.
EMPLOYEE
HANDBOOK

A Staffer's Guide to

SUCCESS, PROFIT, and Eternal SALVATION

Inside George W. Bush's

Executive Branch

BY THE WRITERS OF WHITEHOUSE.ORG

John A. Wooden

Andrew Bradley

John DeVore

Chris Harper

A PLUME BOOK

PLUME

Published by the Penguin Group

Penguin Group (USA) Inc., 375 Hudson Street, New York, New York 10014, U.S.A.

Penguin Books Ltd, 80 Strand, London WC2R 0RL, England

Penguin Books Australia Ltd, 250 Camberwell Road, Camberwell, Victoria 3124, Australia

Penguin Books Canada Ltd, 10 Alcorn Avenue, Toronto, Ontario, Canada M4V 3B2

Penguin Books India (P) Ltd, 11 Community Centre, Panchsheel Park, New Delhi–110 017, India

Penguin Books (N.Z.) Ltd, Cnr Rosedale and Airborne Roads, Albany, Auckland 1310, New Zealand

Penguin Books (South Africa) (Pty) Ltd, 24 Sturdee Avenue, Rosebank, Johannesburg 2196, South Africa

Penguin Books Ltd, Registered Offices: 80 Strand, London WC2R 0RL, England

First published by Plume, a member of Penguin Group (USA) Inc.

First Printing, February 2004

10 9 8 7 6 5 4 3 2 1

CIP data is available.

ISBN 0-452-28519-4

Printed in the United States of America

Set in Trade Gothic, Poster Bodoni, Bembo, and Trajan.

To Antonin, Clarence, Sandra, Tony, and William—
with passionate Gratitude from the entire company.

WWW.CHICKENHEAD.COM

PRESENTS:

A JOINT EFFORT FROM

www.whitehouse.org

www.landoverbaptist.org

www.bettybowers.org

ACKNOWLEDGMENTS

The authors would like to thank the following individuals for their extraordinary support: Giles Anderson, Kelly Notaras, Mark Pace, Brooks Talley, Anna Liza Bella, Kat Kinsman, Chuck Graef, Amber Tozer, Gary Brozek and the entire gang at Plume, Andrew Celli, Chris Dunn and everyone at NYCLU, our inexplicably loving parents, and most importantly—Mr. David S. Addington, Counsel to the Vice President of the United States of America. We couldn't have done it without you!

CONTENTS

I.
INTRODUCTION

MEMORANDUM

WHITE HOUSE, INC.
WASHINGTON

TO: _____
FROM: President George W. Bush
RE: Heartfelt Personal Welcome to
Aforementioned Valued Employee

Dear Staffer:

A big Texas HOWDY and congratulations on not being the last little sissy who didn't get picked for the most righteous, most all-American kickball team in the history of mankind. If you are holding this book, you've already seen the welcome video ("Surveillance & Secrecy: Learning from the Amateurism of Nixon"), and you can bet your last upper-upper-class-white-collar dollar that either you or someone in your bloodline worked for my daddy—or owes him a favor.

So welcome aboard, because even though I may never actually speak to you, that doesn't mean I don't consider you to be like kinfolk. And please, don't worry about how you can possibly repay my family for accepting you into our dynasty's sweet, blessed bosom. Some day, and that day may never come, my mom will call upon you to do a service for us. But until that day—accept this dreary government gig as a lesser opportunity to prove your submissive allegiance to the Bush Thousand-Year Reign!

In His Name,

George W. Bush

George W. Bush
President & CEO, White House Inc.

P.S. – Good luck on the sodium pentothal Q+A!

Surviving Our Nation's Fetid Capital

White House Inc. appreciates the fact that all of its staffers have selflessly abandoned their happy and whole-some lives deep in America's well-scrubbed heartland. Relocating to a city infested with a shocking variety of brown-skinned subhumans, prancing homos, and stores conducting business on Sundays is a sacrifice we all make together.

With its iconic marble memorials, grand, tree-lined avenues, and ghettoized population of Capitol Hill shoe pol-ishers addicted to CIA-grade crack, Washington, D.C., is a bit like the biblical Sodom. It is beautiful as you gaze down through your bulletproof helicopter window, but on the inside, the city is a teeming intestinal slurry of degenerate Socialists and crooked liberal bureaucrats.

As Republicans, we endure the agony of prolonged submersion in this not-quite-partisan-enough cesspool for one reason: to serve as an obstacle to the passage of any legislation that doesn't trigger avalanches of green-backs to cascade over us and our closest corporate supporters. Without our steadfast efforts, our beloved Red States (referred to hereinafter as "The Real America") would be at the mercy of baby-slaughtering hedonists who want nothing more than to split our hard-earned trust funds with the lazy, the stupid, and the sinisterly pig-mented, and dole out K-Y-slathered vibrators to mongrel retarded children to get them so worked up, they'll breed a whole race of welfare-worshipping Hillary groupies.

Throughout your tenure here, you will find it useful to think of the White House as the glorious Alamo—an impenetrable fortress under seige by hostile, indigenous dirt people. Today, just like our courageous Texas fore-fathers, we too are fighting the God-ordained fight against the surrounding army: bloodthirsty pacifists, antipol-lution crazies, free-press traitors, human-rights sickos, the unsaved, the unwashed, the unconnected, and throngs of filthy street people contaminating our public toilet seats with crab lice and AIDS. But unlike Alamo heroes Davy Crockett, Jim Bowie, and John Wayne, who valiantly used a Christian building to kill as many taco-slinging illegal aliens as they could, we *shall* prevail!

Team Bush Philosophy

The Liberating Freedom to Submit and Obey

Remember—there is no "I" in "plutocracy." That is why, in all matters concerning your so-called liberty to make personal decisions that affect your life, White House Inc. bases its approach on the Texas High School Cheerleaders Association's time-tested method for instilling starry-eyed conformity in each of their silicone-engorged teen warriorettes. Like them, you too are free to wantonly jiggle your freshly waxed political coochie with simulated abandon. Please be advised, however, that in modeling itself on a sport fueled by crystal meth and bovine-growth hormone, this company will also brutally punish you and your family if you deviate even slightly from the carefully choreographed messages—whose verbatim regurgitation is now your sole reason for living.

Replacing Big Left-Wing Government with Even Bigger Right-Wing Government

As a member of this administration, you must publicly sing the praises of a small federal government and take care to promote the pleasant, arguably constitutional concept of "states' rights." Company policy on this matter basically boils down to this: as long as states are willing to do only what our CEO thinks is right, we leave them alone. If, however, willful states refuse to debase themselves before the ideological altar of our most ferociously conservative check-writers, the issue of states' rights becomes one of states' *wrongs*. In all such cases, it becomes necessary to impose federal mandates so sweepingly draconian, we make Big Government Democrats look like a bunch of chicken-dancing hippy anarchists.

☆ **EXAMPLE: If a state wishes to haul a pack of retarded shoplifters and elderly, back painkiller junkies before a firing squad in the cafeteria of a voucher school built atop a toxic waste dump, we quietly wash our federal hands of the situation. But if an otherwise "sovereign" state permits abortion, euthanasia, or the matrimonial sanctioning of hot man-on-man ass sex, we'll be on their backs quicker than Whitney Houston can snort a kilo of dandruff off a random stagehand's shoulder.**

Creating Men Equal Did Not Stop God from Playing Favorites Later On

As all patriotic citizens know, it says right there in the Constitution (or the Declaration of Independence) that America's official mascot, God, created all men equal. Fortunately for Republicans, your parents' money and business connections quickly laid waste to the Lord's suspiciously Socialist agenda. A man may start out as an indistinguishable blob of phlegm stuck to the clammy wall of some silly woman's uterus, but if you think American men remain equal after elbowing their way out of the womb, simply flag down any of your new coworkers.[1] They will be happy to regale you with their personal "How my daddy saved my ass from serving with the rednecks and coloreds in Vietnam-or-Gulf-War-1" story.

Our Sworn Duty to Us

White House Inc. is a closely held corporation. Its employees are stockholders whose financial fortunes as future war profiteers and influence peddlers will rise and fall like Bill Clinton's penis in a receiving line— depending on the success of the enterprise. The voters, of course, are our easily gulled customers. Outside of the very wealthiest, voters receive absolutely *no financial benefit whatsoever* from our infrequent but well-publicized endeavors. To our collective amusement, polls confirm that most Americans remain completely oblivious to our rather conspicuous contempt for them, no matter how often we ignore them in favor of our corporate and religious benefactors. Indeed, during your tenure here at White House Inc., you will enjoy balling a metaphoric fist and forcefully slugging the middle class in its eager snout over and over again, only to watch it come running back for more, tail flapping merrily like an affable golden retriever puppy. Remember: it doesn't really matter if Americans actually buy the products we sell, just as long as they feel a warm tingling in their loins each time they see our star-spangled advertising (See Photo-Op Protocols—p. 166).

---

[1] Not including your CEO's personal servant, Colin Powell (he's the Negro not wearing a dress).

DID YOU KNOW?

We Represent the "Middle of a Road" (The Road Just Happens to Veer Wildly to the Right)

In a consumer-oriented society like America, it is important to tell voters what we are selling before they find out otherwise for themselves. Remember: every slogan that White House Inc. supports is "mainstream"—even if appropriated without alteration from constituents who can routinely be found armed to their remaining teeth and holed up in a Montana militia's prayer bunker. Similarly, we are "conservatives," not "right-wing zealots." Surprisingly however, "conservative" played better in seven out of ten focus groups than "fascist" (although the three dissenting votes invariably comprised our most fervent supporters).

II.
ORIENTATION
MATERIALS

We've done our best to make Orientation as enjoyable as possible—whether you're one of them red Chineses or not!

EMPLOYEE INFORMATION FORM

Fill out this form in its entirety. While it requests no new data about your person beyond what has already been collected on your fifty-page job application, it nevertheless remains an essential component of White House Inc.'s strict emulation of corporate human-resources methodology.

Full Christian Name: _____

Born: _____-_____-_____ (mm-dd-yyyy)

Born Again: _____-_____-_____ (mm-dd-yyyy)

Photo:

Circle one only. If you are of mixed race, use a No. 2 pencil to soot up your skin and kink your hair so security will recognize you. (Orientals may use yellow crayon or highlighter.)

EMPLOYEE INFORMATION FORM (cont.)

Position:

West Wing:

❏ Cabinet/Reelection Staff

❏ Secretary of War/Campaign Event
Planning

❏ Policy/Christian Mysticism

❏ Elocution Therapy/
Texas-Twang Coaching

❏ Administrative/Absentee-Ballot
Processing

❏ Speechwriting/Scriptural-Apho-
rism Recitation

❏ Legal/Document Disposal

❏ Secretarial/Brew Master

❏ Intern/Chastity Embodification

❏ Homeland Security/Hysteria Czar

❏ Public Events Management/Cine-
matography

❏ Media Relations/
News Corp. Conduit

East Wing:

• **First Lady**

❏ Hand Servant/Compliment Special-
ist

❏ Crisis Stabilization/Pharmacist

❏ Mixologist/Blender master

❏ Wardrobe/Sears Liaison

❏ Tobacconist

❏ Botox Consultant

• **First Twins**

❏ Tutor

❏ Party Planner

❏ Trust-Fund Comptroller

❏ Tattoo/Genital-Piercing Adviser

❏ Horticulturist

❏ Bail Bondsman

Plant Operations:

❏ Security/United States Secret Service

❏ Kitchen/Chi-Chi's Master Chef Exchange Program

❏ Chauffeur/Pickup-Truck Detailing

❏ Groundskeeping/Mexican Relations

❏ Custodial/NAACP Outreach

EMPLOYEE INFORMATION FORM (cont.)

Pay Class:

❏ <$1,000,000/year (not including vocational kickbacks)

❏ >$1,000,000/year (including book advances and any speaking fees over four figures)

Associations:

Academic:

❏ Yale University

❏ Bob Jones University

❏ Harvard University

❏ Lee Atwater Bipartisan Prep

❏ Andover Academy

❏ Southern Millionaire's University

❏ The Barry Goldwater Montessori

❏ Texas A&M

❏ Homeschooled

Fraternal:

❏ Sigma Chi

❏ DEKE

❏ Skull & Bones

❏ Gamma Omega Pi

❏ Kappa Kappa Kappa

❏ Other (Traditional)

❏ Other (Coed/Pussy Frat)

Social:

❏ Loyal Order of Skinned Owl

❏ Federalist Society

❏ "Friends of Bill W"

❏ Sons of the Confederacy

❏ Christian Coalition

❏ Al-Anon

❏ Augusta National Golf Club

❏ Moral Majority

❏ National Rifle Association

❏ American Yachtsman

❏ Operation Rescue

❏ Brotherhood of Simulated CEO Scruples

❏ National Creation Science Foundation

❏ Concerned Women Against Uppityness

EMPLOYEE INFORMATION FORM (cont.)

Professional:

- ❏ American Nukular Society
- ❏ Coal Technology Association
- ❏ American Petroleum Institute
- ❏ American Logging Conference
- ❏ United States Chemical Council
- ❏ National Mining Association
- ❏ U.S. Defense Contractor Coalition
- ❏ National Association of Religious Broadcasters
- ❏ The WTO Wholesale Exploitation Alliance

Faith:

- ✔ Christian (Bible-Believing Protestant)
- ❏ Other/False-God Worshipper

Sexual Orientation:

- ❏ Normal
- ❏ ~~Homo~~

Signature: _____

Date: _____

Thumbprint: Place indelible-ink left thumbprint in the box below, and use a piece of Scotch tape to affix a lock of nonpubic hair and/or toenail clipping suitable for DNA analysis.

PROOF OF OVERT PATRIOTISM
WORKSHEET

While as a newly hired employee of White House Inc., your personal background has already been rigorously vetted, further testing is necessary to determine whether you might be someone with a soft spot for peace, a Benedict Arnold corporate whistle-blower, or an after-hours packer of fudge.

Full Christian Name: _____

Social Security #: _____-____-_____

Place of Birth:
- ❏ United States of America
- ❏ Other/Godless Wasteland

Are you now, or have you ever been, a member of the Democratic Party? Y | N

Organized Team Sports Played:
- ❏ Varsity Football
- ❏ Varsity Baseball
- ❏ Intramural Greco-Roman Hot-Oil Wrestling
- ❏ Armed Forces Active-Duty Evasion

Vegetarians are traitors to the American way of life. T | F

PROOF OF OVERT PATRIOTISM WORKSHEET (cont.)

Indicate which of each of the decals below are prominently affixed to your domestically produced SUV(s):

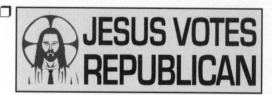

* Available in the White House gift shop.

PROOF OF OVERT PATRIOTISM WORKSHEET (cont.)

Favorite movie:

❐ *Rambo*

❐ *Red Dawn*

❐ *Top Gun*

❐ *Independence Day*

❐ *Birth of an Anal Nation* (Clarence Thomas Special-Edition DVD)

The South lost.   T │ F

"Allied" foreign countries whose goods you actively boycott:

❐ Canada

❐ Russia

❐ Turkey

❐ Germany

❐ France

❐ Massachusetts

❐ San Francisco

❐ Mordor

The Pledge of Allegiance was secular tripe for 180 years

before the words "under God" were added by Congress in 1956

during the noble Red Scare: F │ F

By signing below, I hereby relinquish my right to habeas corpus and all other supposed rights afforded me by the former so-called Bill of Rights. Furthermore, I acknowledge that the Department of Homeland Security, the Department of Justice, and/or the FBI may use this information to arrive at the conclusion that I am some kind of pinko, commie, freedom-hating homo freak who deserves a steel-tipped federal jackboot ass-kicking, so help me John Ashcroft.

SIGNATURE: _____

DATE: _____

SKULL & BONES
SECRET REAFFIRMATION PLEDGE

I, _____, as a member in good standing of the sacred SKULL & BONES fraternal order, do solemnly swear to honor and uphold Bonesmen traditions and values during my entire tenure at White House Inc. As a privileged child of American royalty, a token minority, or a mind-bogglingly nouveau riche contributor to the GOP who has been retroactively inducted into this secret Ivy League pyramid scheme, I pledge the following:

- To obey Skull & Bones OVER God & Country (whatever our CEO may say in speeches to the malleable public notwithstanding).
- To dress in black velvet robes and deliver violent paddlings to the trembling exposed buttocks of my brothers.
- To never reveal, even under threat of death, that the U.S. Constitution was written as an elaborate satire of the Age of Enlightenment run amok (except for that part about blacks only being worth three-fifths of white people).
- To never allow persons of low investment portfolio balances into our Greenwich mansions, country clubs, sacred tree houses, inner sanctums, government offices, GOP presidential tickets, or circle-jerk pajama parties.
- To always provide unmarked cash, ornamental boards of director placements, sloppy seconds, insider information, military spoils, and juicy government bureaucrat posts to anyone who gives the secret Skull & Bones "elephant walk" handshake.

I shall forever uphold the Holy Trust placed in me by my Skull & Bones brothers. If ever I should fail in this pledge, may I be stripped of my membership and mink-lined ritual undies, my yacht sunk, my Swiss bank accounts emptied, and may all of my porcelain-skinned daughters be ravaged by swarthy, insatiable ethnics, forever sullying and scrambling my genetic code and dooming my progeny to a life of public schools, police stops, pre-fab housing, and trawling for bargains in the Wal-Mart double-discount aisle.

Amen, and tap the keg.

Signed: _____   Date: _____

BENEFITS OVERVIEW

 White House Inc. offers competitive federal benefits (unavailable in the private sector) including health, life, and afterlife insurance coverage, complimentary monogrammed handgun lockers, and opportunities for nearly unimaginable financial advancement through post–White House tell-all book deals, your own cable-news talk show, outlandish speaking fees, or simply marketing your perceived influence to corporations that would rather pay lobbyists than class-action settlements. These benefits help ensure that you and your family enjoy an added measure of security in the highly unlikely event that your platinum parachute fails to deploy correctly.

MEDICAL COVERAGE: All White House Inc. personnel are assured the best, most economical medical coverage available. As such, each employee will find the following in their comprehensive coverage packet: (a) an Ontario driver's license, (b) a Canadian passport, (c) a Canadian health card, and (d) a stack of round-trip plane tickets to Toronto.

PSYCHIATRIC COVERAGE: Your health-coverage package has been carefully designed to focus exclusively on nonimaginary conditions and diseases. Everyone knows that *real* sickness is limited to things you can see, like runny noses, angry chancres, and Oliver Stone movies. Ever since the days of Mary Todd Lincoln, the GOP has steadfastly refused to validate the liberal, fuzzy science myths of "depression"—whether physiological or fiscal in nature. So should you come to mistakenly believe that you are experiencing symptoms of so-called mental illness, you stand strongly advised to make like a butt-sniffing Armed Forces sodomite, and clam up about it.

★ **NOTE: The phenomenon of "hearing voices" inside the White House complex should NOT be interpreted as the onset of schizophrenia. That's just the good Lord delegating His will to us—His personal, handpicked administrators of the planet Earth.**

REPRODUCTIVE HEALTH: The official policy of White House Inc. is that if you are female and want a choice, go to Blockbuster. No matter that it's been more than thirty years since a liberal Supreme Court caved in to Gloria Steinem's Back-Talking Bitch Brigade and made it legal for teen sluts and raped joggers who were just asking for it to get painless abortions in clean hospitals, instead of being taught a good lesson by having some colored witch doctor jam a rusty fishing hook up their cooter. In this White House, we embrace Almighty God's will that no lowly woman should have an ounce of self-determination once she's got a hoo-hoo full of sacred man jelly. Of course, inasmuch as our domestic morality policy is applicable only to those too poor to get around it, you remain free to accept any familial offers to spirit you off by private Lear-jet® to some hellish pit like Japan where they don't think twice about Ginsu®-slicing the womb boogers right out of you.

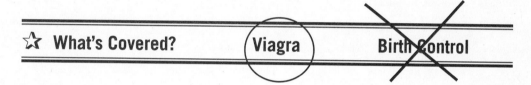

☆ **What's Covered?** (Viagra) Birth ⨯ Control

MATERNITY LEAVE: If you have so little consideration for the schedules of your more diligent male (and barren female) workers that you persist in going forward with the delivery of an infant, special arrangements are in place to accommodate your selfishness. A clearing has been made behind Mrs. Bush's prize American Beauties in the Rose Garden for you to emit your offspring into the hands of the First Lady's handmaid, Rosa Hernandez. Rosa will chew through the umbilical cord, place your child into a clean, one-gallon plastic mayonnaise tub, and provide several Kleenex for wiping your lady parts clean. You may then return to your workstation until the end of the day, at which point Momma's little tax deduction may be retrieved from its comfy bed of peat moss in the soundproof toolshed. Oh, and congratulations.

WORKERS' COMPENSATION: As a Republican, you understand that any injury you incur in the workplace is at your own risk and in no manner whatsoever the responsibility of White House Inc. As such, if any injury befalls you that renders you less than 100 percent able to perform your job, we are also confident that you will observe our policy of workers' compensation by compensating for this lack of work with a prompt resignation. Corporate Security will clean out your office and incinerate anything interesting.

DRUG TESTS: As a former National Guard airman who forfeited His right to fly a plane rather than risk His right to fly without one, your President feels empathetic toward those of you who have certain chemicals coursing through your veins that you do not wish to reveal to nosy people in white lab coats. Nevertheless, all people who enter the White House (other than the President and His extended family—including Noelle Bush and her personal entourage of Eckerd cashiers) must provide a fresh urinalysis sample each after-noon. To make this daily obligation as painless and convenient as possible, Styrofoam coffee cups will be placed at each workstation during lunch hour so that your flow of urine need not interrupt your flow of work. When leaving for the day, please label your cup clearly and place it carefully on either of the floor trays flanking Spotty and Barney's water bowl.

SUBSTANCE-ABUSE REHABILITATION: If an unexpected arrest leads you to believe that you may have an inconvenient dependence on any substance, you are expected to deal with the situation swiftly and dis-creetly. First, notify the Bush family's private counsel of the name of the judge assigned to your case so a determination can quickly be made if he is susceptible to the gentle persuasions of phone calls from gov-ernors of very populous Southern states. Next, choose a specific date to claim as the last time you were a user and a loser. Whatever date you pick (and make sure it is in the *past*), commit it to memory or write it on your cuff so that scheming reporters won't trip you up on television. This will help you, years hence, to keep your story straight in your compelling denial: "Through the strength of Jesus, I've learned from mis-takes I may or may not have made. And I'm not going to get into what drugs I may or may not have done _____ years, _____ months, and _____ days ago!"

VISION: Your vision benefits are provided through the generosity of the al-Faisal branch of the al-Saud royal family. As a condition of your right to collect such benefits, you are required to turn a blind eye to any transgressions by Saudi Arabia and its citizens that may lead directly to a few—or even a few thousand—deaths of Americans. The President is confident that, like Him, you will agree that this is a rather small price to pay for free horn-rimmed glasses in perpetuity.

DENTAL:

EMPLOYEES WHOSE POSITIONS MANDATE CAMERA TIME: Your White House Inc. dental plan ensures that you will have the confidence that comes from having a camera-ready set of choppers at all times. Rather than squandering policy funds on experimental dentistry procedures such as fillings, cleanings, and root canals that are often indiscernible to the viewers at home, you have the option of either covering your crooked, mossy dentition with glistening ceramic veneers or going whole hog by selecting from a beautiful collection of dipped-wood uppers and lowers from the patriotic George Washington collection.

EMPLOYEES WHO DO NOT APPEAR BEFORE CAMERAS AS PART OF THEIR JOB: Unlimited complimentary extractions are performed by Corporate Security in the break room every Wednesday from noon to 12:15 P.M., and may be preceded by two (2) anesthetic tequila shooters.

RETIREMENT: In addition to other benefits, you may look forward to a lucrative post in the Carlyle Group immediately upon leaving White House Inc. There, you will encounter the extravagantly compensated ranks that have included George H.W. Bush, James Baker (the man who spearheaded the President's fight against the pernicious influences of the popular vote) and former investors such as the bin Laden family, all of whom have made vast personal fortunes by exploiting the policies set in place by Republican White Houses. There is, of course, no shame in such influence marketing, for why should only your backers get richer when there is so much taxpayer money to go around?

AFTERLIFE: Through programs such as mandatory Bible study and full-body emersion baptisms in the South Lawn fountain, management ensures that your employment benefits extend beyond mere mortal life. How can the value of personal salvation be measured, you ask? Well, thanks to the diligence of the Human Resources Department, White House Inc. accountants have taken a stab at it. The results of their complex actuarial formula will be reflected on your biweekly pay stub, under the 30 percent withholding heading "Eternal Security Plan."

DEATH BENEFITS: See "Resignation."

DIVERSITY TRAINING

WHITE HOUSE, INC.
WASHINGTON

White House Inc. is a corporate environment that takes pride in practicing a conservative approach to diversity training. Rather than waste the taxpayers' money on politically correct "awareness curricula," our CEO believes it is more effective for employees to stumble across representations of America's ethnocultural mongrelization in their everyday work environment. Use the check boxes below to track your exposure to diversity reminders here in White House Inc.'s headquarters.

- ❏ "Naked Nubian Mammy Riding a Leopard" Velvet Painting
- ❏ Navajo-Comanche-Apache "Calico Injun Scalp" Patchwork Shag Rug
- ❏ Hot Wheels Toy Car Exhibit: Flaming, Lowrider El Caminos of the Puerto Rican Ghetto
- ❏ Oriental "Ching Chong Karate Fu" Figurine & Charlie Chan Chicken Chow Mein Chopstick Set
- ❏ Arabic "Allah Akbar" Gilded, Scale-Model, Crude-Oil Drilling Platform
- ❏ Antique Santa Anna Mexican Wispy Mustache Fork Groomer
- ❏ First Lady's Johnny Mathis Pinto Pony Skin-Covered Scrapbook
- ❏ Michael Flatley "Lord of the Dance" Animatronic Lawn Leprechaun & Guinness Sprinkler

President Bush is totally comfortable with billionaire coloreds. (Copyright © AFP/ Corbis.)

By signing below, I indicate that I have visited and experienced each of the White House diversity reminders listed above. I am now more acutely aware of the larcenous and sexually promiscuous hoards of peculiar people with whom Real Americans are currently forced to share their lovely country.

SIGNATURE: _____

DATE: _____

I have no idea where some of these minority types got the foolish idea into their nappy heads that they are supposed to come to America to celebrate their cultural shortcomings instead of trying to blend in. Goodness gracious me, America is called a melting pot—not a salad bar! Sometimes, I want to grab those quaint little people by their stooped shoulders and say, "Make like the Wicked Witch of the West—and melt already!"

MANDATORY OPERATION TIPS PARTICIPATION

WHITE HOUSE, INC.
WASHINGTON

While employees of White House Inc. are exempt from adherence to most federal guidelines, statutes, and laws, your participation in all *administration-conceived* programs and initiatives is still required. As part of President Bush's domestic policy crown jewel "Operation TIPS," all staffers are automatically deputized as Homeland Security personnel and are required to complete as many copies of the Official Anonymous Lead Form as may be required to focus the searing light of justice on every last terrorist and/or America-hating miscreant in our great nation.

ANONYMOUS LEAD FORM

Instructions: Use this form to report any and all suspicious persons you may encounter to the proper authorities. Simply provide information below, and drop the completed form into any mailbox. No postage is required.

Suspected Terrorist Information:

Suspect's Name: _____

Suspect's Address: _____

Description (check all that apply):

❏ Raghead	❏ Allah Lover	❏ Atheist
❏ Liberal	❏ Democrat	❏ Vegetarian
❏ Homo	❏ Artist	❏ Welfare Mother
❏ Intellectual	❏ Environmentalist	❏ Immigrant
❏ Falafel-Breath	❏ Sand Negro	❏ Camel Jockey
❏ Pro-Choicer	❏ Gun-Control Nut	❏ Academic
❏ Feminazi	❏ ACLUer	❏ Pacifist
❏ Homeless		

Suspect is stockpiling chemical, biological, and/or nukular arms:

❏ Yes   ❏ Maybe

FINDING YOUR WAY AROUND: WHITE HOUSE FLOOR PLANS

In light of the previous occupant's penchant for spewing bodily fluids with no discernible regard for intended targets, the White House mansion has been extensively reupholstered, refurbished, and optimized for habitation by the Bush family. Familiarizing yourself with the following maps will not only streamline your servitude, but also help you avoid the indignity of being beaten senseless by the Secret Service for straying into restricted areas and/or rubbing the President's mother the wrong way.

ACCESS ZONES: Eye-level doorjamb plaques indicate the clearance required to gain access to each room in the White House Inc. complex. Please note authorization levels listed below:

☞ **NO ACCESS**—All sectors (except Laura's Gift & Curio Shop) are closed to Voters Who Complain, Foreign Terrorists, Congressional Democrats

☞ **PUBLIC**—Open to Tour Groups, Janitorial Staff, Congressional Republicans

☞ **RESTRICTED**—Open to Authorized White House Personnel, Cabinet and Other Senior Administration Staff

☞ **VIP ZONE**—Open to Executive Inner Circle, Trusted Lobbyists, Pioneer-Level Campaign Donors

☞ **TOP SECRET**—Open to Extended Bush Family, Presidential Prayer Team, Defense Contractors, Saudi Arabians, Halliburton Accountants, Ranger-Level Campaign Donors

---

OLD MANSION: GROUND FLOOR

CLASSIFIED
REFLECTS 2001 RENOVATIONS

~~Vermeil~~ Fancy Non-French Gold-Plated Room

~~China~~ Non-Oriental Communist Plate & Saucer Room

Diplomatic Reception Room

Map Room

Jefferson Davis American Heritage Drawing Room

Center Hall

Library

Spiro Agnew Broom Closet

Grand Staircase

Gubernatorial Records Crypt

Applebees® Home-Cookin' Kitchen

Ceremonial Entry Hall

FOX News On-Site Studio

Security Operations

Stockade

White House Physician

POINTS OF NOTE:
1 = Foreigner Delousing Dip & Baptism Station
2 = Tim LaHaye & Jerry B. Jenkins *Left Behind* First Editions
3 = First Lady's Precious Moments® Hutch
4 = Crusade Planning & Strategy Board
5 = Democratic Campaign HQ Listening Post
6 = Shoulder-Mounted Rat Storage Units
7 = "Rough Rider" Electric Bull
8 = Complete Works of Danielle Steele
9 = Canine Cuisine Preparation Area
10 = First Twins Cuisine Preparation Area

KEY
= 10 Commandments Plaque
= Pretzel Barrel
= Spittoon
= Soft Money Receptacle
= Gift Kiosk
= Handgun Locker
= Treadmill
= Prayer Spot
= Ciggie Break Area
= Wet Bar
= Self-Serve Pharmacy
= Kennebunkport Red Phone
= Clinton Fornication Stain
= Photo Op (Charges Apply)

OLD MANSION: MAIN FLOOR

CLASSIFIED
REFLECTS 2001 RENOVATIONS

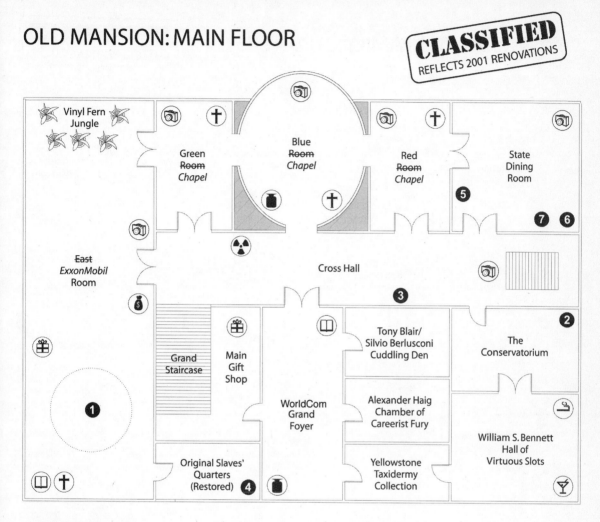

POINTS OF NOTE:

1 = *Hee Haw* Line Dancing Pen
2 = Ronald Reagan Model Choo-Choo Platform
3 = Thomas Kinkade® Fine Art Exhibit
4 = Secretary Powell's Cot
5 = First Lady's Avocado Fiestaware® Showcase

6 = Hungryman® Dumbwaiter
7 = "Gravies of the World" Buffet

KEY

= 10 Commandments Plaque

= Pretzel Barrel

= Spittoon

= Soft Money Receptacle

= Gift Kiosk

= Handgun Locker

= Treadmill

= Prayer Spot

= Ciggie Break Area

= Wet Bar

= Self-Serve Pharmacy

= Kennebunkport Red Phone

= Clinton Fornication Stain

= Photo Op (Charges Apply)

OLD MANSION: FAMILY QUARTERS

CLASSIFIED
REFLECTS 2001 RENOVATIONS

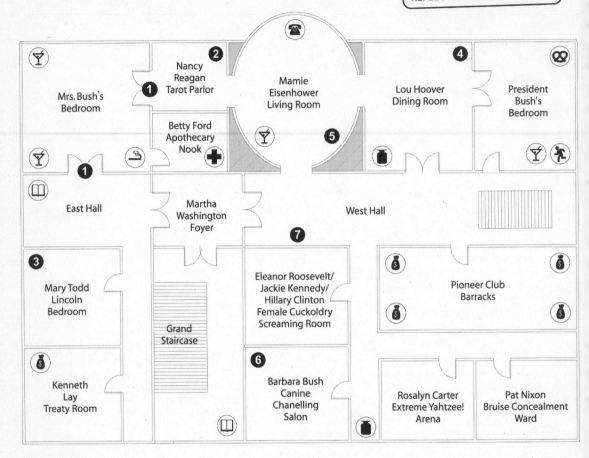

POINTS OF NOTE:

1 = Connubial Overture Prevention Gate
2 = "Do Be Do Be Do Me" Sinatra Hideaway Bed
3 = ATM Machine
4 = "Let Them Eat Cake" Buffet
5 = Presidential X-Box® Nook

6 = Nancy Reagan Dart Board
7 = Amway® West Hall Toiletry & Detergent Bazaar

KEY

= 10 Commandments Plaque	= Gift Kiosk	= Ciggie Break Area	= Clinton Fornication Stain
= Pretzel Barrel	= Handgun Locker	= Wet Bar	= Photo Op (Charges Apply)
= Spittoon	= Treadmill	= Self-Serve Pharmacy	
= Soft Money Receptacle	= Prayer Spot	= Kennebunkport Red Phone	

WEST WING: MAIN LEVEL

CLASSIFIED
REFLECTS 2001 RENOVATIONS

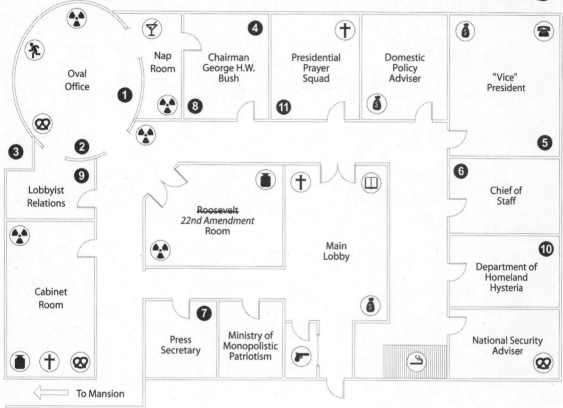

Oval Office

Nap Room

Chairman George H.W. Bush

Presidential Prayer Squad

Domestic Policy Adviser

"Vice" President

Lobbyist Relations

Roosevelt 22nd Amendment Room

Main Lobby

Chief of Staff

Cabinet Room

Department of Homeland Hysteria

Press Secretary

Ministry of Monopolistic Patriotism

National Security Adviser

← To Mansion

POINTS OF NOTE:

1 = Dissention Trapdoor
2 = Hooked on Phonics Geography Flash Card Cabinet
3 = Rose Garden Pig Roast Pit
4 = Pork Rind Sampler Bar
5 = Nukular Launch Button
6 = Spotty & Barney's Newspaper Latrine
7 = Helen Thomas Flammable Effigy
8 = Jennifer Fitzgerald Foldout La-Z-Boy®
9 = ATM Machine
10 = Gallup & Zogby Terminals
11 = Chick Tract Vending Machine

KEY

= 10 Commandments Plaque	= Gift Kiosk	= Ciggie Break Area	= Clinton Fornication Stain
= Pretzel Barrel	= Handgun Locker	= Wet Bar	= Photo Op (Charges Apply)
= Spittoon	= Treadmill	= Self-Serve Pharmacy	
= Soft Money Receptacle	= Prayer Spot	= Kennebunkport Red Phone	

CLASSIFIED
REFLECTS 2001 RENOVATIONS

WEST WING: MEZZANINE LEVEL

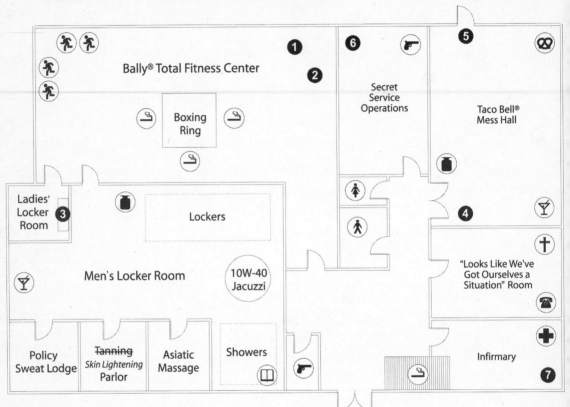

POINTS OF NOTE:

1 = Nautilus Machines
2 = Free Weight Machines
3 = Cubby Holes / Wetwipe Dispenser Unit
4 = Presidential Cheetos® Snack Bar
5 = Colored Entrance
6 = Phone to VP's Office/Ambulance
7 = Auto-Amputation Table

KEY

= 10 Commandments Plaque	= Gift Kiosk	= Ciggie Break Area	= Clinton Fornication Stain
= Pretzel Barrel	= Handgun Locker	= Wet Bar	= Photo Op (Charges Apply)
= Spittoon	= Treadmill	= Self-Serve Pharmacy	
= Soft Money Receptacle	= Prayer Spot	= Kennebunkport Red Phone	

WEST WING: BASEMENT LEVEL

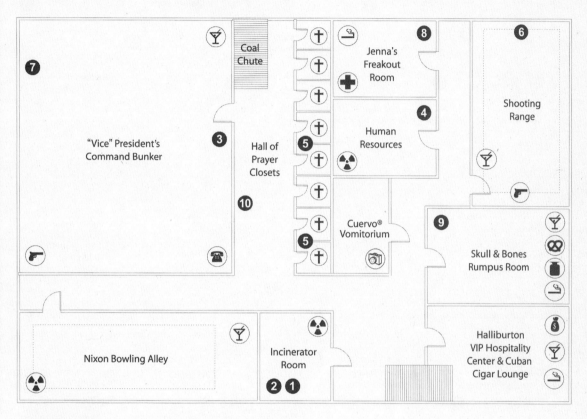

Coal Chute

Jenna's Freakout Room

Shooting Range

"Vice" President's Command Bunker

Hall of Prayer Closets

Human Resources

Cuervo® Vomitorium

Skull & Bones Rumpus Room

Nixon Bowling Alley

Incinerator Room

Halliburton VIP Hospitality Center & Cuban Cigar Lounge

POINTS OF NOTE:

1 = Document Furnace
2 = Suggestion Box
3 = Pacemaker Charger
4 = Thumbscrew Polygraph Unit
5 = Glory Hole
6 = Wall of Democrats
7 = Air Force One Control Panel
8 = "World of Hookahs" Islamic Understanding Zone
9 = Escort Service Database
10 = Leviticus Chapter 20 Plaque

KEY

= 10 Commandments Plaque
= Gift Kiosk
= Ciggie Break Area
= Clinton Fornication Stain

= Pretzel Barrel
= Handgun Locker
= Wet Bar
= Photo Op (Charges Apply)

= Spittoon
= Treadmill
= Self-Serve Pharmacy

= Soft Money Receptacle
= Prayer Spot
= Kennebunkport Red Phone

EAST WING

CLASSIFIED
REFLECTS 2001 RENOVATIONS

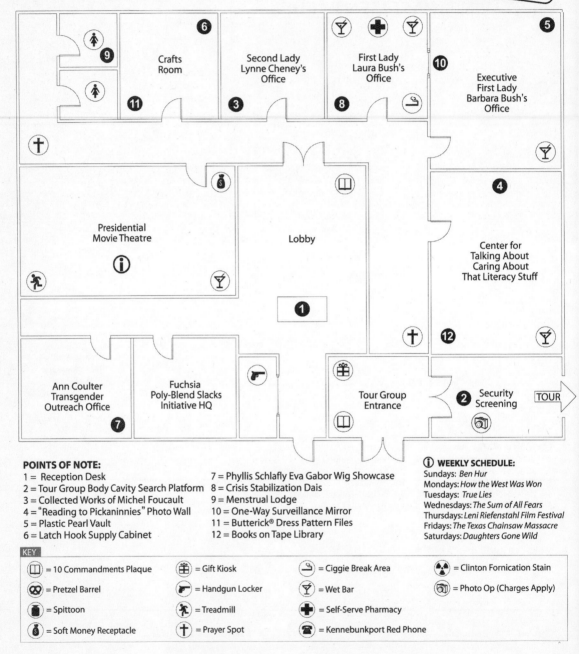

Crafts Room

Second Lady Lynne Cheney's Office

First Lady Laura Bush's Office

Executive First Lady Barbara Bush's Office

Presidential Movie Theatre

Lobby

Center for Talking About Caring About That Literacy Stuff

Ann Coulter Transgender Outreach Office

Fuchsia Poly-Blend Slacks Initiative HQ

Tour Group Entrance

Security Screening

TOUR

POINTS OF NOTE:

1 = Reception Desk
2 = Tour Group Body Cavity Search Platform
3 = Collected Works of Michel Foucault
4 = "Reading to Pickaninnies" Photo Wall
5 = Plastic Pearl Vault
6 = Latch Hook Supply Cabinet
7 = Phyllis Schlafly Eva Gabor Wig Showcase
8 = Crisis Stabilization Dais
9 = Menstrual Lodge
10 = One-Way Surveillance Mirror
11 = Butterick® Dress Pattern Files
12 = Books on Tape Library

ⓘ WEEKLY SCHEDULE:
Sundays: *Ben Hur*
Mondays: *How the West Was Won*
Tuesdays: *True Lies*
Wednesdays: *The Sum of All Fears*
Thursdays: *Leni Riefenstahl Film Festival*
Fridays: *The Texas Chainsaw Massacre*
Saturdays: *Daughters Gone Wild*

KEY

= 10 Commandments Plaque
= Gift Kiosk
= Ciggie Break Area
= Clinton Fornication Stain
= Pretzel Barrel
= Handgun Locker
= Wet Bar
= Photo Op (Charges Apply)
= Spittoon
= Treadmill
= Self-Serve Pharmacy
= Soft Money Receptacle
= Prayer Spot
= Kennebunkport Red Phone

III.
SENIOR MANAGEMENT

GEORGE W. BUSH
President & CEO

As both the President and CEO of White House Inc., George W. Bush brings a whole lifetime's experience of having sprung from the loins of a long line of entitled million-aire politicians. A native of blue-blooded New Haven, Connecticut, Mr. Bush was born July 6, 1946, to parents Barbara Pierce Bush and future President George H.W. Bush. George W. would go on to spend much of His prepubescent youth in the Wild West frontier outpost of Midland, Texas, amassing stock in His father's lucrative petroleum concerns, getting to know powerful family friends in Houston's buzz-killing criminal justice system, and luxuriating in the local children's culture of homogeneity, plentiful assault rifles, and after-school cockfighting tournaments.

Patterning His life after His father's, Bush attended three of America's most exclusive institutions of higher learning. During high school at wildly expensive, but in no way "elitist," Philips Andover Academy, Bush eschewed the effeminacy of reading and study to throw Himself more fully into the giddy world of male cheer-leading. Later, at Yale, He fought a dogged campaign to capture the presidency of the Delta Kappa Epsilon fra-ternity, from whose vomit-splattered basement He would pursue such scholarly interests as the American history of collegiate hazing, foosball, and a blessedly short-lived engagement to Miss Cathryn Lee Wolfman, whom as the stepdaughter of a Hell-bound Jew, was clearly unfit for conjugal service in a burgeoning political dynasty. In 1968, Bush earned His bachelor's degree from Yale, graduating in the top 85 percent of His class.

During the utterly necessary Vietnam War, while so many of His leftist, America-hating peers took the path of least resistance—passive conscription and recreational gook slaughter in the balmy Agent-Oranged jungles of Southeast Asia—Bush instead bravely volunteered to jump to the front of the Texas Air National Guard wait list. There, His genetic predisposition to leadership was quickly acknowledged with a fabulously rare special com-mission to second lieutenant, rightfully catapulting Him past the stiflingly bureaucratic folly of Officer's Training

School. A devoted patriot, Bush quickly mastered the controls of His obsolete F-102 "Delta Dagger" fighter jet, dominating the skies of the Lone Star State's front lines and defending countless pregnant women and helpless kittens from sorties of Eastern Airlines' tactical "whisper jets." So exemplary was His militarism, in fact, Bush saw fit to reward Himself with a twelve-month AWOL vacation prior to being granted a special honorable discharge in the fall of 1973.

Shortly thereafter, and despite having been rejected from the University of Texas Law School, Bush matriculated at the less selective Harvard Business School, whose wizened administrators were capable of setting aside their egregiously discriminatory affirmative action program to mine the alumni gold buried deep within His C-strewn Yale transcript. Bush would earn His M.B.A. in 1975, at which time He would joyously bid His final farewell to the stifling, sissyish halls of the Ivy League. After ten bourbon-soaked years at citadels of preppy privilege, so potent was your CEO's distaste for the preening East Coast arrogance of tweed-wearing, womanish academics, He repudiated them by vowing to devote the rest of His life to speaking in a charming accent picked up while watching Roy Rogers films and a touring company production of *L'il Abner*.

Returning to Texas, Bush spent the next fifteen years getting to know American voters by listening to their urgent, if somewhat slurred, concerns, as delivered from orange velour bar stools in scores of Houston's most troubled honky-tonks. To broaden His knowledge of the domestic issue of business failures, He selflessly founded a succession of wholly unprofitable oil companies. This highly formative period saw our leader aggressively leveraging His birthright to secure wave after wave of disposable financing from His father's normally cautious investor friends. In 1990, restless in His role as a generously compensated director of the Harken Energy Corporation, your preternaturally business-minded master had the visionary good sense to coincidentally unload nearly $1 million in stock just days before its share price went into the proverbial pooper.

Flush with millions in wholly fortuitous, non-insider profits, Bush reveled for several years in His dream job as general manager of the Texas Rangers baseball franchise. Then, in 1994, Bush ran for and was elected governor of Texas, narrowly defeating the suspiciously mannish and brassy Democratic incumbent Ann Richards, who once brazenly taunted Bush's father during a telecast of the 1988 Democratic National Convention. Four years later, Bush would reaffirm His victory over the cheap-talking, leather-faced Richards—winning 27 percent of the colored vote and making Texas history as the first governor elected to consecutive four-year terms.

Bush's impressive genealogy soon attracted the hungry attention of the Republican Party's more conservative leaders, who saw in Him an exquisitely named white male and superabsorbent ideological tampon who would generously act as a front for their eager plan to reclaim control of the semen-encrusted Executive Branch. These political star makers told Bush that His running mate would be the wizened Nixon Administration veteran Richard B. "Dick" Cheney, a man famous among Washington, D.C., dinner-table companions for his ability to drink a glass of water while quoting Hermann Göring out of the side of his mouth. With the endorsement of all of our party's most influential extremists, the Bush/Cheney ticket went on to win a man- date-inducing, landslide 5–4 vote in the 2000 elections.

A Cancer, President Bush is married to Mrs. George W. Bush ("Laura"), a former teacher and librarian who devotedly toiled in our nation's Godless and dangerous public schools for over one interminable year until she could ensnare an affluent husband. The Bush family also includes two twin daughters (Jenna and the other one), two dogs (Spotty and Barney), a cat (India), and an armadillo (Wetback).

I'm a uniter, not one of those, you know, dividing up things type of folks. I invite all the many parts that make up the fabulous extreme-right wing in this country, from the fabulous neo-fascists to the fabulous tongue-talking religious zanies, to come together to join me in slamming the hell out of all the centrist and liberal American asswipes we have to share our otherwise fabulous country with.

GEORGE H.W. BUSH ("POPPY")
Chairman

With nearly fifteen years of White House experience under his belt, Chairman George H.W. Bush ("41") is proud to carry the vast wisdom and connections he amassed during his own presidency into this, the uncertain new global theater of the twenty-first century.

41 was born June 12, 1925, in Milton, Massachusetts, to parents Dorothy and Prescott, the latter a U.S. Senator-to-be and an industrious war profiteer. George's early years were typical, happy, all-American ones, filled with horsies, nannies, silver spoons, and patriotic Sundays at the country club. Adolescence would see George Herbert matriculate at the prestigious Phillips Andover Academy, where he would make a reputation for himself as an accomplished baseball player, cha-cha dancer, and Texan impersonator.

On his eighteenth birthday, 41 enlisted in the Navy, becoming the youngest pilot ever to receive his wings. Among his ensuing fifty-eight combat missions against the reviled Japs was one in which he was famously shot down over the Pacific. Adrift and alone on the open sea for six days, Bush killed and ate five great white sharks with his bare hands before sneaking aboard an enemy submarine, bludgeoning the entire Godless crew to death, and taking command of the asphyxiatingly soy-scented vessel. He was closing in on Tokyo to ritually dis-embowel the emperor when he heard the glorious news of the atomic bombings in Hiroshima and Nagasaki that ended the war.

Returning to America a decorated hero, 41 wasted no time in marrying his Teamster uncle's doppelgänger, Barbara Pierce, on whose signature strand of oversize faux pearls he could not help but feverishly nibble like a ravenous coyote. Soon after, his newly blushing bride engorged with child, Bush would claim his birthright: a Yale University undergraduate education. It was in New Haven, in the mahogany-paneled legacy citadel called Davenport College, where Bush would be tapped to join "Skull & Bones." Members of this benevolent charity organization pledge on their immortal souls to honor their secret club over both God and country, and to help one another through life's rough spots—from failed IPOs and depressed per-barrel prices, to immigrant laborer strikes and unrequited nepotism.

Rolling up his sleeves after Yale, President Bush moved to Texas and successfully hand-drilled for reliable energy sources when not skulking for the CIA. Having grown tired of the monotony of wealth and privilege and wishing to put an end to nightly hectoring by his political father over the phone, Bush announced a run for the U.S. House of Representatives in 1967. There, he excelled at striking legislative blows against communism, the meddlesome public accommodations provision of the 1964 Civil Rights Act, and disregarding the acid-drenched whining of a rising generation of long-haired sodomites. In 1970, Mr. Bush suffered an unacceptable loss in a race for the Senate to slick and oily Lloyd M. Bentsen, Jr., for which complete revenge remains to be fully exacted.

In 1980, impressed with Bush's wholly accurate declaration that nuclear wars are completely winnable, Ronald Reagan enthusiastically tapped 41 to join him in his victorious presidential bid against the Ayatollah-rimming James Earl Carter. Despite the best efforts of John F. Hinkley, Jr., Bush would remain as Vice President from 1981 to 1989, during which time he and Reagan would snatch America back from the jaws of dangerously progressive thinking. In the process, they would expand the federal bureaucracy to Democratic wet-dream proportions, then magically run it on "Budget Deficit Dollars," thereby turning an overregulated welfare state into a corporate-friendly, tax-free wonderland, and saving the livelihoods of tens of dozens of affluent Children of the Revolution.

> *Having yourself some of those competitive-type sons can get pretty ding-donged trying sometimes. If we give George the presidency for Christmas one year, we can count on little Jebber to be looking for the same gosh-darned thing under the tree eight years later. Fortunately, with Neil, it only takes a billion-dollar taxpayer bailout once in a while.*

Successfully winning twice with Mr. Reagan, Mr. Bush had learned a valuable lesson about American politics: voters are more likely to elect you if you are running with someone good-looking. Therefore, he ordered his campaign committee to scour the nation's golf courses for a hot-looking, but not too-tall Ken doll unfettered by the burden of ideas. And so, with the absolutely, positively, not-Downs-afflicted

J. Danforth Quayle at his side in 1988, Bush would run election night circles around the nasal-voiced Greek dwarf Michael Dukakis, assume the presidency of the United States, and *finally* get to drop-kick the imperious Nancy Reagan through a Pennsylvania Avenue manhole.

Over the next four years, 41 would both topple communism and forever guarantee the loyalty of a little-known Muslamian colony called "Kuwait." But despite wildly high approval ratings, and thanks solely to the putrid economic seeds sown by tax-and-spend liberal Jimmy Carter twelve years earlier, a recession took root, which people had the ungrateful gall to point out.

Determined to teach the voters a lesson on how bad things could get under the malaise of a Democratic president's economic policies, Bush took the responsible route and did nothing. Furthermore, having grown tired of needing to constantly dry-clean her blue dress with white polka dots for formal occasions, Barbara Bush began to lovingly berate and badger her husband to move back to Houston. 41's retort of "Read my lips. No more Texas!" was misconstrued by inattentive journalists and ultimately ignored by Mrs. Bush. Yet in the end, purely out of admiration for his lovely wife, President Bush voluntarily stepped down from power in 1992, inadvertently triggering the complete moral collapse of our Christian nation.

Eight years later, enraged by the dangerous riptides of peace and prosperity sweeping away innocent Americans, the Lord called Bush out of the Carlyle Group for a triumphant return to the White House (accompanied by his prodigal son, George W.). The President, well rested, has shown himself eager to tackle new challenges, including the recently invigorated Arabiac and Soviet menaces and a foolhardy national preoccupation with the myth of "energy conservation."

Chairman Bush is a Gemini. He likes foreign policy, pink lemonade on a hot day, speed golf, movies without hanky-panky, and scolding Jewish reporters.

RICHARD "DICK" CHENEY
"Vice" President

Born on January 30, 1941, in Lincoln, Nebraska, Richard Bruce Cheney was raised in Casper, Wyoming, by his parents Richard H. and Marjorie Cheney. A robustly handsome and popular boy whose future was apparent, young Dick was voted "Most Likely to Become CEO of a Multinational Conglomerate Whose Business He Knows Nothing About" by his classmates at Robert E. Lee Senior High School.

Later, Cheney would win a scholarship to prestigious Yale University, but upon finding the academic culture there to be cliquish and self-congratulatory (in that especially unbearable New England way), Cheney would boycott his classes. In time, Yale officials would come to believe that Cheney's academic performance was too poor to justify his continued enrollment and would ask him to leave. Little did they know that the joke was on them—that Cheney's apparent "failure" was in fact a brilliant protest against the inherently diseased nature of Ivy League intelligentsia. Cheney returned to Wyoming, where he would earn his bachelor's and master's degrees in political science—among people capable of forming opinions of him based on more than any conspicuous contempt for so-called debate and didacticism.

██

██████████████████████████████████████ his first position as a special assistant

in the Nixon Administration ███████████████████████████████████████

███

mod In 1978, Cheney would run successfully for Wyoming's lone seat in the U.S. House of Representatives.

██

██

After the 1992 voluntary departure from office of George H.W. Bush, Cheney would enter the private sector for a number of years before becoming Vice President. Specifically, he served as CEO of Halliburton Corporation, the world's largest oilfield services and products company. There, in the interest of his future need for bipartisan cooperation, he would dispense with his long-standing contempt for government regulation and subsidies—successfully winning over $3.8 billion in federal contracts and taxpayer-insured loans on behalf of Halliburton's understandably impatient and deserving stockholders.

As Vice President, Mr. Cheney assumes the role of the CEO should President Bush ever be rendered unable to perform his duties, whether due to absence, illness, hangover, shin splints, abject ineptitude, and/or being Raptured to Glory.

> *Television is making it harder and harder for us ugly guys in politics. That's why I ended up down the ticket from an irritable frat boy who has no clues, but great hair. Fortunately, working for President Nixon all those years taught me that you don't have to be pretty to be powerful. Dick also showed me that you don't have to be scrupulous either—just careful. On balance, that lesson's come in even handier lately!*

The very picture of cardiological resilience, Dick Cheney is married to his high school sweetheart, Mrs. Dick Cheney. Mr. Cheney's star sign is Aquarius. He enjoys movies, low-impact walks in the park, conflicts of interest, and collecting all manner of contemporary evangelical pamphlets.

JESUS
Commander of the Commander in Chief

Jesus' last name is "Christ," and contrary to secular tradition, He has no middle initial. He is the first (and, after all the drama, only) Son of God (much as George W. Bush is the first son of President George Bush). Indeed, having a father who thought he was God is only one providential way that our President's life follows in the sandal prints of His pal Jesus. Just as Jesus' Father had a steady job that was shrouded in mystery and involved killing lots of evildoers, President Bush's father worked for the CIA. In marked contradiction to their staid, passive-aggressive fathers, neither the young Jesus nor George W. seemed able to hold down a job. In fact, there are many years in both men's lives that are completely unaccounted for and the subject of much speculation. Some say that Jesus went to India; most say that George W. went to Tijuana. When He returned to town, Jesus developed quite a reputation for being a drunk (Matthew 11:19). In devoted emulation of His Personal Savior, George W. Bush did everything in His power to gain a similar standing in Midland, Texas.

Like your current President, Jesus and His Dad also ended up holding the same title, and even had the same jobs. Currently, Jesus and His Daddy live in a big mansion up in Heaven. Like the President, Jesus takes orders from His Father, even if it means some folks have to die. Jesus and President George W. Bush became best friends when Mr. Bush was going through a period of wild adolescence. He was forty. Jesus came to him and said, "The first step to giving up booze is just telling reporters that you have stopped." Grateful for this useful insight, George raised a profound and emotional toast to His new Personal Savior. Ever since that libation-soaked evening at the Lucky Coral Tavern, Jesus and George found out they have much in common. They even agree that people who don't agree with every word they say are evil, wrong, and going straight to Hell.

Jesus was born into the family of a poor Jewish carpenter in a small town in Bethlehem in either 4 B.C. or around A.D. 6 (depending on whether you are a Matthew or Luke fan). He spent time as a traveling preacher for many years until He answered a Jerusalem classified ad for a "Son of God and the Jewish Messiah." Jewish folks got real ticked off about that because they expected the Messiah to come down from Heaven with special effects and big Hollywood production values. They were so mad about someone as scruffy as Jesus having the audacity to call Himself their Messiah that they had Him killed. Well, they didn't expect Him to jump out of His grave like a zombie three days later, nor did they expect Him to float off to Heaven like an untethered balloon at the Macy's Thanksgiving Day Parade. But He did! It's a historical fact you can read about in His autobiography, the Holy Bible. Jesus now discreetly makes his services available only in invisible form, eschewing the showy personal appearances His mother makes on dirty windows and taco shells for the benefit of easily impressed Catholics. It is He who guides the President's hand in every decision that affects the lives of the only people He genuinely cares about—affluent, conservative Christian Americans who love wars.

Jesus is a Capricorn. He likes camel-leather footwear, omnipotence, pumping iron with Pat Robertson, and dictating new company policy to the President's secretary.

Remember that I love you unconditionally, but if you don't love me back and give me 10 percent of your money every Sunday, nothing will delight me more than drop-kicking your worthless ass into the torture pit of Hell for all eternity!

MRS. GEORGE W. BUSH ("PICKLES")
First Lady

When describing First Lady Mrs. George W. Bush ("Pickles"), it is appropriate on countless levels to defer to the superior psychophysical summary offered by her husband, President George W. Bush: "She doesn't try to steal the limelight." Indeed, Mrs. Bush is in many ways most noteworthy for her intensely admirable inclination to allow her husband to methodically overshadow each and every element of her unfortunately female being. Such is the way and the path of a goodly Republican First Lady.

With a plaintive face that seemed inspired by the dusty prairies of bucolic Texas, Laura Welch was born in Midland, Texas, on November 4, 1946. The daughter of a carpenter father and a housewife mother not unlike Joseph and Mary themselves, Laura learned early to happily adhere to the traditional gender roles that would one day make her an object of feverish desire for Stetson-wearing alpha males. A popular girl, Laura blossomed in high school into an accomplished dancer and enthusiastic consumer of the fine, life-affirming tobacco products of the RJ Reynolds Tobacco Company. In the fall of 1963, Laura narrowly averted a life of pointless obscurity when she ran a stop sign and collided with another vehicle, inflicting a fatal neck fracture on Mike Douglas, a reputedly serious boyfriend not genetically affiliated with an oil-drenched political dynasty.

Following the accident, fifteen years passed inconsequentially until Laura made the acquaintance of her destined betrothed—George W. Bush. Recalling her first impressions of the future Commander in Chief, Laura told *The Washington Post* in March 2001, "I thought he was fun. I also thought he was really cute. George is very fun. He's also slightly outrageous once in a while in a very funny and fun way and I found that a lot of fun." Just over five weeks later, Laura accepted his fun proposal of marriage. Several years later, Laura would reluctantly submit to marital congress with her husband, whose turbo-charged, future-President seed would promptly deliver two hard-drinking Bush twins to her intensely fertile, all-American womb.

As only the second First Lady in history to hold a postgraduate degree, Mrs. Bush will spend the duration of her husband's two terms in office resolutely focused on the politically nonvolatile issue of juvenile literacy. She will visit 237 primary and secondary schools, where she will deliver easily comprehensible speeches extolling the virtues of reading. Occasionally, she will be photographed either holding or smiling at one or more carefully prescreened black children. Mrs. Bush is often joined in these exploits by Mrs. Dick Cheney. Both are managed and disciplined at White House Inc. by Mrs. George H.W. Bush.

> *As a Republican, I take time to talk about how important family is. That's why abandoning my daughters to campaign during their all-important senior year of high school didn't stop me from telling local TV morning shows in thirty states how precious those girls are to me.*

A Scorpio, Mrs. Bush's hobbies include reading, saying she reads, honoring and obeying her husband, pretending to be a nurturing and supportive matriarch for her spirited twin daughters, keeping a detailed birding journal, not aspiring to noteworthy achievements independent of her husband's, and all kinds of other stuff about reading.

MRS. GEORGE H.W. BUSH ("BAR")

Executive First Lady

A veritable whirling dervish of matriarchal magnetism and fork-tongued wit, Mrs. George H.W. Bush brings a special brand of maturity and silver-haired spunk to the otherwise somber and heretofore ignored position of Executive First Lady. A perennial role model for the husky drag-queen set, Bar (as she's known to those who know her best) can light up a room with her trademark flurries of urgent directives and stinging criticisms.

(Copyright © Bettman/Corbis.)

Born June 8, 1925, in Rye, New York, to Pauline and (future McCalls publisher) Marvin Pierce, the Pre–Mrs. George H.W. Bush enjoyed a respectable and modestly comfortable youth. Refined and tactful from the very moment of conception, Bar held elementary-school tea parties that were the stuff of legend, replete with handpicked Barbados cherry scones, Tiffany cup and saucer sets, and the doting attentions of her Darjeeling-native hand servant, Takdah. Generous sometimes to a fault, Bar was quick to invite even the most common neighbor girl to the frequent slumber parties in the hayloft of her Acropolis-inspired pony stable.

Bar would weather the Great Depression bravely while attending a succession of exclusive boarding schools, including Rye Country Day and South Carolina's Ashley Hall—the latter's Christmas dance being where she would stalk future President George H.W. Bush until he finally succumbed to her playful taunts about his masculinity. Within two years, the two were engaged to be married.

The decades passed quickly, and Bar sired a sizable menagerie of Bush children while George H.W. made his rapid climb up the political ladder. Relocating to wherever her husband's noble freedom-fighting took them became a way of life, and, as such, Bar's beloved wedding furniture suffered untold nicks and scratches over the course of twenty-nine moves between George's first election to the U.S. Congress and his inauguration as Vice President under Ronald Reagan.

When President Bush was finally and justly elected President, Bar reinvented what it means to be the First Lady, eschewing the gratuitous slimness of decades of predecessors and reveling in her queen-size magnificence. Her first term as First Lady would see Bar coauthor two best-selling books with her beloved springer spaniel, Millie, and succeed (albeit only in the final hours) at eliminating the overpowering and stubbornly lingering scent of Nancy Reagan's Chanel No. 5 from the First Lady's East Wing toiletry alcove.

After President Bush voluntarily stepped down in 1992, with her children long since grown and moved away, Bar luxuriated in eight years' worth of free time, mastering the collected works of Sir Andrew Lloyd Webber for the zither, and at long last pursuing her lifelong desire to become an unrivaled master of seashell picture-frame crafts.

But that was then. Today, with Executive President George H.W. Bush back at the helm of the White House, Bar is busier than ever before, tasked with the day-to-day oversight and management of both Mrs. George W. Bush and the more headstrong Mrs. Dick Cheney, who might otherwise selfishly engage in activities of interest to themselves.

I love all of my children equally. That's why I constantly have to ratchet down my affection for all of them when one of the losers disappoints me or marries a willful rhymes-with-punt who threatens to write a tell-all book.

Mrs. George H.W. Bush's star sign is Gemini. She likes movies, going out for dinner, walks on the beach, like-minded Caucasian Christians, and leaders of the free world with a sense of humor.

(Copyright © Bettman/Corbis.)

MRS. RICHARD CHENEY ("LYNNE")
Second Lady

Mrs. Dick Cheney was born Lynne Ann Vincent on August 14, 1941, in Casper, Wyoming. The daughter of a ruggedly masculine sheriff and her deferentially demure, erudite husband, Lynne took an early and girlishly appropriate interest in those aspects of American art and culture that are so comfortably reminiscent of eighteenth-century tradition and thought. An insatiable reader of books, the young, future Mrs. Dick Cheney took a special liking to the tragically romantic works of the Frenchman Victor Hugo, most notably his seminal novel *The Hunchback of Notre Dame,* from whose dog-eared pages she would take her inspiration when selecting a mate.

After earning her bachelor of arts degree in English literature from Colorado College, the not-yet–Mrs. Dick Cheney found herself still without a breadwinning spouse. Wisely hedging her bets, she took refuge in postgraduate education, earning both a master's degree and PhD in the pointedly nonpractical, yet supremely lady-like, academic province of poetry studies. Fortunately for pre–Mrs. Dick Cheney, a life of scholarly spinsterism was narrowly averted, when one fine July evening in 1964, she would cross paths with Yale dropout Dick Cheney, an old high school acquaintance with whom

> *As an ambitious girl growing up on the desolate prairies of Wyoming, I always prayed to Jesus to give me something none of my friends has. Well, wouldn't you know it, the Joker went and gave me a lesbian daughter!*

she'd never had occasion to spend an evening of spirited fellowship in the back of his father's Rambler. The two would dine together the next evening at a romantic restaurant popular for its waitstaff on rollerskates, then venture out for a night of doing the twist between sloe gin fizzes. Two weeks later, they were married in an intimate, drive-through ceremony at a Las Vegas motor chapel. Mrs. Dick Cheney would go on to disgorge two daughters, one of whom would fulfill her Godly obligation to couple with men. The other of whom is still invited to come home for Thanksgiving—*hopefully alone.*

It was spending time with Pat Nixon— serving our wonderful husbands of the same first name and fondness for Jews—that taught me that not everyone who seems vacuous or distant is; often, they are just schnockered! I realize now that getting comfortable around a First Lady like Pat, so unburdened with intellectual curiosity, was wonderful training for my current role as America's female second banana.

In the years that have passed, Mrs. Dick Cheney has evolved into a prolific and prominent author. Her works include *Telling the Truth* (Simon & Schuster, 1995), a book exposing the disgusting practice of universities not telling the warm, wonderful story of America's noble ascension to jealously regarded perfection, *Kings of the Hill* (second edition, 1996), a dishy, insider's take on Newt Gingrich's seemingly preordained rise to rule with an iron toupee, and her personal favorite opus, *Sisters* (Signet, 1981), a Western romance novel celebrated at womyn-only folk festivals for its steamy depictions of brothel activity, sapphic coitus, and powerful statement on the putrescence of masculine anatomy relative its vegetable garden competition.

Americans can be proud to have a Second Lady like Mrs. Dick Cheney, even if her vocal political activism does invoke the specter of Hillary Rodham Clinton—the grotesquely bossy and opinionated former First Lady whose sickening noncookie-baking example has corrupted untold millions of little girls into walking away from their God-intended lives of barefooted pregnancy to become uppity feminazis.

For the duration of the Bush Administration, Mrs. Dick Cheney will studiously endeavor to never take the limelight away from her more taciturn superior, Mrs. George W. Bush. Together, and under the stern management of Mrs. George H.W. Bush, these paragons of conjugal subservience are devoted to tackling a host of important issues, including but not limited to the promotion of juvenile literacy, fighting the proliferation of offensively bourgeois china patterns, and preventing the shame and heartbreak that comes from planting colorful perennials not suited to one's climate zone.

Mrs. Dick Cheney's star sign is Leo. She likes R-rated movies, Infusium 23 shampoo, postmodernist interpretive dance, and playing second fiddle.

KEY PERSONNEL

Chief of Staff

Reports to: President & CEO

Primary Responsibilities: Manages West Wing employees, prepares President's daily schedule, wakes President from morning and afternoon naps, serves as the President's liaison to the East Wing during all times He is on the First Lady's "Dog Doo List"; reminds the President before public appearances about whether He's supposed to look sad or happy; maintains ability to preserve absolute secrecy (even under threat of severe genitorture—or, worse—impoverishment).

Specialty Areas: Preparing attendance reports, willingness to reduce oneself to the status of middle-aged houseboy at a moment's notice, enforcing break-room cleanliness, enduring near-constant sarcastic put-downs from immediate superior, providing routine grooming services to First Canines (including nail clipping, manual anal-gland expectoration and dingleberry removal), biding time until accepting seven-figure advance for post–White House partisan memoir.

Attorney General

Reports to: The Lord Jesus

Primary Responsibilities: Protects America's white adults, children, and womb-dwelling, peanut-size gummi people from all manner of terrorists, homos, terrorists, feminists, terrorists, the ACLU, terrorists, titillating photography, terrorists, teen crack dealers, terrorists, foreigners, terrorists, statuary nudity, terrorists, civil liberties, terrorists, Martha Stewart, terrorists, campaign-finance reformers, terrorists, atheists, terrorists, and all other liberal personifications of evil (terrorists).

Specialty Areas: Indefinitely detaining and/or deporting brown-skinned kebab-munchers; preparing private citizen no-fly lists; derailing colored judge nominations; jingoistic crooning; overcoming the crushing humiliation of losing elections to corpses.

NOTE: Familiarity with the Constitution is not a requirement and may indeed disqualify an applicant.

National Security Advisor

Reports to: Northrop Grumman, Karl Rove

Primary Responsibilities: Using fuzzy fluorescent balls and the Oval Office Velcro® map of the world, delivers the daily Oval Office CliffsNotes® security briefings that provide the President with an exhaustive knowledge of which defenseless Muslamian nation is, unbeknownst to even them, harboring super-secret death rays that can fry the entire Eastern seaboard of the United States; assists in passing off the inevitable defeat of an impotent foe as a glorious victory over a wicked and powerful enemy.

Specialty Areas: Maintaining an iron mental grasp on the sociopolitical landscape of opportunities to flex mad U.S. military-industrial muscle; acting as White House point person with the CIA for any documentation that needs to be created to justify a war when the actual reasons are either classified (election related) or stem solely from the President's personal animus; fetching coffee.

Budget Director

Reports to: The Forbes 400, Karl Rove

Primary Responsibilities: Conducts tireless analysis on the back of an envelope to eliminate wasteful spending in the United States budget so that average Americans can enjoy year-end tax savings large enough to splurge on breakfast for one at Denny's; at the same time ensures that needy Fortune 50 corporations have sufficient tax breaks to set up executive retirement accounts sheltered from the avarice of bankruptcy courts and underwrite the purchase of newer, more elegantly paneled Gulfstream jets—lest board members be forced to suffer the indignity of sharing a fuselage with people they don't even know.

Specialty Areas: Ability to courageously apply the 100 percent accurate label "PORK BARREL INSANITY" to such worthless expenditures as Social Security, Medicare, highway maintenance, and public education; slashing all funds for any other program that is close to the hearts of people who spurn us when we let them get near the polls; diving into piles of gold doubloons wearing a top hat and monocle.

Press Secretary

Reports to: Rupert Murdoch, Karl Rove

Primary Responsibilities: Interfaces with the three corporations that own all domestic and international news media to help create the illusion that White House Inc. wishes the people of America to know what it is doing; answers softball questions lobbed by a cowering press as a surrogate for a President without visible talents for expressing Himself lucidly, thinking extemporaneously or, due to his debilitating ADD, not forgetting the question before He has finished making up an answer; to obfuscate reality through the dissemination of a repetitive mantra of painstakingly crafted pleasantries and half to one-quarter truths.

Specialty Areas: Evading direct questions, maintaining ability to concentrate and remain lucid—even while asphyxiating in an impenetrable fog of Helen Thomas's sour halitosis.

OTHER POSITIONS AT A GLANCE

Office:	Reports to:
Domestic Policy Advisor	Heritage Foundation, Federalist Society, John Birch Society
Drug Czar	Anheuser-Busch, RJR, Pfizer
U.S. Trade Representative	American Corn Growers, U.S. Steel, WTO
E.P.A. Administrator	Dow Chemical, International Paper, Eastman Kodak
Secretary of Energy	ExxonMobil, Halliburton, Chevron
Secretary of Labor	Kathy Lee Gifford
Secretary of Housing and Urban Development	The Suburban Strip Mall and Negro Containment Foundation
Secretary of Interior	The American Strip-Miner's Council
Secretary of Education	Christian Coalition, Center for Scientific Creation
Secretary of State	Secretary of Defense
Secretary of Veterans' Affairs	GOP Warhawk's Deferment Mentoring Council
Secretary of Homeland Security	Duct-Tape Manufacturers Association, Smith & Wesson
Secretary of Defense	Lockheed Martin, General Dynamics, Northrop Grumman
Secretary of the Treasury	Merrill Lynch, Arthur Andersen
Secretary of Transportation	AMG Hummer, Bell Helicopter
Secretary of Agriculture	Archer Daniels Midland, ConAgra
Secretary of Health and Human Services	U.S. Faith Healers Federation

YOUR SUPERVISOR

Supervisor's Name: _____

Your supervisor is your immediate superior. In other words, he is superior to you in every respect, with the possible, inconsequential exceptions of your experience, education, and skill. He earned his White House Inc. commission as an alleged expert by being a pillar of partisan check-writing fervor, and by clinging with white-knuckled determination to the coattails of someone much more important than him—namely, your CEO's father.

Remember always that your supervisor's public-approval rating is a useful barometer for gauging the quality of your performance. If his ratings are high, you are doing good work, and your supervisor will selflessly preserve your anonymity by enduring the harsh scrutiny of public adulation. Should the public start to perceive him as inept or mendacious, however, you will be hoisted into the gun sights of the bloodthirsty press, where you will atone for your incompetence by claiming sole responsibility for bad intelligence, lapsed judgment, and/or a patriotism so fervent it cannot be dampened by facts. Then you will apologize profusely and beg pitifully to keep your job as an anonymous—and now disgraced—peon.

IV.
RULES &
REGULATIONS

WORKING HOURS

"The early bird gets the insider stock tip."—*Poor Harken's Almanac*

One important aspect of your transition from the private sector to White House Inc. will be the difficult adjustment to the concept of "working hours." In Corporate America, where you were probably a Senior Vice President or even a CEO, your workweek would have been limited to twenty to twenty-one grueling hours, including business helicopter ski trips to Aspen, scotch-soaked brainstorming meetings in the Bellagio high-roller lounge, and important tenth-hole merger negotiations at Chewton Glen. But here at White House Inc., we reluctantly demand the appearance of implied labor for a full forty hours each week. Of course, this doesn't mean you have to actually *accomplish* anything. Unless you are a gardener, an elevator operator, President Bush, or one of those hunchback banditos who scrub toilets with their prosthetic hooks, you really have nothing to worry about as long as you are sitting in your cubicle with your computer on.

White House Inc. Work Hours*

M–F:　7 A.M.–5 P.M. (with three forty-five-minute naps**)

Sat:　7 A.M.–4 P.M. (with two PlayStation breaks of durations required to win**)

Sun:　9 A.M.–10 A.M. (church***)

10:30 A.M.–4 P.M.

Though these hours may feel excessive at first, remember that in exchange for your gray-collar toiling, you will now be able to tap into the aphrodisiac of raw power your old-boy connections and six-figure campaign donations have finally placed within reach. And though waking up before the tooth fairy may be burdensome, it will all seem worthwhile once you've had a chance to rewrite the tax code, snicker at a business competitor's FBI file, or hand your blue-eyed children a three-billion-dollar construction project in an oil-rich principality that owes us, as the Vice President might say, "Big time!"

---

　* All times are subject to change and extension without notice and *do* add up to forty hours (trust us).

　** Not applicable to workers not occupying the Oval Office.

　*** Non-Christians are exempt from joining in on the hymns and, indeed, from returning to work ever again.

Logging Your Hours

Because we implicitly trust our excruciatingly screened employees, you'll find no time clock at White House Inc. There's something better: a secure company intranet featuring state-of-the-art time-tracking software. Simply sign in with your name and pass code at the beginning of each workday, then log your time—in fifteen minute increments—using the intuitive interface of drop-down menus to indicate which Special Interest Group or Political Action Committee you are lovingly fellating at any given time.

Overtime

In the event of national catastrophe, sliding approval ratings, or—Jesus and President Bush willing—intimations of the Rapture, you will be expected to remain within the White House complex and work overtime. This may mean putting in a few extra hours of your regular duties, or it may mean special duties, such as shredding documents for days on end in Mr. Cheney's "Magical Black Hole of Secrets," or appeasing the mercurial God of polling by draining the blood of your first-born son into the Apocalyptic Survival Tanks of the subterranean Masonic ziggurat.

BREAKS

Coffee: Your CEO knows that coffee is the second-best picker upper to ever come out of Colombia. It keeps us alert and energized to do our jobs. As such, each employee is encouraged to take up to fifteen coffee breaks per day—which are also wonderful opportunities to get to know your fellow employees better. So when you find yourself in need of a little R&R away from all that silly government busywork you pretend to do, simply mosey on down to the main dining hall, where at any time of day or night you'll find scores of your colleagues happily loitering around the dispensers of delicious, piping-hot Kroger®-brand percolator coffee—just chatting, laughing, and swapping fish tales, bawdy spic and jigaboo jokes, and even the occasional trophy wife.

Cigarettes: Feel free to take as many cigarette breaks as your lungs may require to remain refreshed, relaxed, healthy, and mentholy fresh. But please remember that the way you hold your cigarette is very important. Men should clasp the base or filter (NOT "butt") of the cigarette firmly between the thumb and index finger. Gals should gently clamp the midsection of the cigarette between their fully extended and impeccably manicured, if somewhat yellowed, index and middle fingers. Only French whores blow smoke out their noses. Please understand that a failure to adhere to gender-specific tobacco norms can be *very* dangerous! You would hate to cut short a long life of enjoying nonaddictive tobacco due to being frantically bludgeoned in a fit of gay panic by Senator Santorum.

"Now I lay me down to sleep..."

Prayer: The speed of one's advancement up the White House Inc. corporate ladder is directly commensurate with the frequency of one's conspicuous prayer breaks. Indeed, anywhere you go inside the White House complex, you will encounter pious clusters of coworkers fervently reciting Scripture in plain sight of the nearest audio-enabled security camera. Also, many chapels and prayer closets are available to you, all of which feature glass doors as it is administration policy that there is little point in praying if someone can't see you do it. On those rare occasions when you feel the need to talk to the Lord Jesus without others listening, please use these facilities. Jesus has a very busy schedule, so you will want to check His appointment calendar in Human Resources before closing your eyes and begging for things, otherwise you might just end up praying into the air.

☆ **A Note of Caution: All new staffers stand advised to exercise extreme caution when citing biblical teachings that might perversely mock company policy—such as turning the other cheek, eschewing material possessions, loving your enemies, not judging people, and praying for those who hate you.**

Adult Beverage: You must take two adult beverage breaks per day, which combined should not exceed 240 minutes. The Adult Beverage Break Room is managed by interns recruited from President Bush's college fraternity, DKE. Its theme is "Hell Week," and you are required to enjoy it. Indeed, whether you're funneling righteous sixers of Mickey's Big Mouth with a whooping posse of poli-sci majors, or being force-fed Jägermeister Jell-O shots as you spiral into a fabulous alcohol blackout, you'll enjoy a relaxingly nostalgic trip back to the days when your own fraternity brothers employed camaraderie-building threats of physical violence and social ostracism to browbeat you into publicly masturbating onto a stale saltine.

☆ **NOTE: Please be respectful and allow a half hour before and after prayer breaks before consuming unconsecrated adult beverages.**

Poopy: Time is money, and money is time. As corporate team players, we strive to avoid squandering valuable company time on personal matters. Indeed, whether it be making doctor appointments, pandering to the demands of newborn offspring, or the tedious task of extruding your daily allotment of solid waste, White House Inc. asks that you attend to all personal matters only late at night and on weekends. That said, should digestive imperative require that you take a poopy break during work hours, we ask that you adhere to all posted safety guidelines (See Restrooms—p. 76), limit break duration to two (2) minutes or less, and demonstrate common sense in your choice of reading material (e.g., *National Review, American Spectator, The Love Sonnets of Ted Nugent, Christianity Today,* and the print edition of *NewsMax.com*).

Arm Wrestling: Arm wrestling has a long and proud tradition at White House Inc. During its heyday early in President Bush's first term, each afternoon saw dozens of free weight–chiseled staffers lining up to challenge Senior Adviser Karen Hughes, who remained undefeated up through her final day on the job. Today, manly employees from every department still enjoy friendly, spontaneous arm-wrestling breaks throughout the building. To find matches already in progress, listen carefully for the telltale sounds of grunting and celebratory expletives. Alternately, you may initiate a new arm-wrestling break yourself by rolling up your right sleeve, flexing your biceps, and bellowing, "Okay, which one of you palm-tickling pansies wants to wrassle for a rack of ribs at the Arlington Morton's? Loser buys!"

Tardiness

You are expected at your desk for morning prayers by 7:00 A.M. sharp. Immediately thereafter, you are to be on the phone attending to the needs of potential campaign contributors. Tardiness will not be tolerated by senior management and is punishable by written reprimand from the Chief of Staff, long-term loss of influence peddling privileges, and/or having to deliver meals-on-wheels to Bob Dole.

THE PRESIDENT'S SCHEDULE

All business at White House Inc. revolves around the comings and goings of our CEO, George W. Bush. You will find that familiarizing yourself with His standard weekly schedule (subject to change at a moment's notice) will be of considerable use in the execution of your day-to-day duties. His itinerary is provided here for your convenience. Please bend your life to fit.

Sundays

Morning:

8:00—	3 Miles on Treadmill
9:00—	Church
11:00—	Policy Review w/ Karl
11:08—	Velveteen Bunny Snuggle Time on Oval Office Settee

Afternoon:

12:00—	Fund-Raising Lunch
1:30—	Photo Op w/ Colored Children
2:00—	Microsoft Solitaire
3:00—	Nap
5:00—	Cuticle Trimming

Evening:

7:00—	Church
8:00—	Watch TiVo of *The O'Reilly Factor*
9:00—	"Laura Time" or "Little Dubya Time"
9:12—	Bed

Mondays

Morning:

8:00—	Jazzercise
9:00—	Prayer Squad
10:00—	"Bipartisan" Strategy Meeting
10:30—	Refreshment Break
10:30—	Real Strategy Meeting

Afternoon:

12:00—	Lunch w/ Dr. Bill & Dennis
1:00—	Bill of Rights Reform Brainstorming
3:30—	Nap
5:00—	Leak Rumors to Matt Drudge and Cindy Adams

Evening:

8:00—	Bible Study
9:00—	"Barney & Spotty Time"
9:20—	Bed

Tuesdays

Morning:

8:00— Trampoline Aerobics

9:00— Prayer Squad

10:00— Public Speaking Tutor

Afternoon:

12:00— Heritage Foundation Lunch

1:30— Bin Laden Family Courtesy Call

3:00— Nap

5:30— Flash Card Geography Lesson w/ Condi

Evening:

8:00— Document Shredding

9:00— "First Twins Time" Conference Call

9:10— Bed

Wednesdays

Morning:

8:00— "Sweating to the Oldies" Step Class

9:00— Prayer Squad

10:00— Telephone Mano a Mano
w/ Karen Hughes

11:00— Teleprompter Rehearsal

Afternoon:

12:00— Petrochemical Billionaire's
Club Luncheon

1:30— Cabinet Meeting

2:00— Xbox

3:00— Nap

5:30— Investment Portfolio Review

Evening:

7:00— Wednesday-Evening Worship Service

8:00— Narcotics Anonymous

9:00— "Poppy & Momma Bar" Call

9:10— Bed

Thursdays

Morning:

8:00— Thighmaster

9:00— Prayer Squad

10:00— Weekly Status Report Due on
Cheney's Desk

11:00— Armor All Tires of Air Force One

Afternoon:

12:00— Online Adult Education Seminar
at Bob Jones University

1:30— Offshore Holdings Review

3:00— Nap

5:30— Webcam Circle Jerk w/ Tony Blair
& Silvio Berlusconi

Evening:

6:00— Dinner & Gravy Boat Levitation
with the Falwells

8:00— Line Dancing in the East Room

9:00— Rose Garden Kegger

11:45— Bed

Fridays

ESPN Day—Camp David

Saturdays

ESPN2 Day—Crawford, TX

HOLIDAYS

White House Inc. observes the formal holidays indicated below. Though our offices are closed for business on these days (as well as nuclear snow days), you will receive full pay. If a paid holiday coincides with your paid vacation or leave time, you may add another day to your paid time off. Similarly, if a holiday should fall on a Saturday or Sunday, you will be paid to take off Friday or Monday, respectively. In short, so long as you're not dead, it's difficult to imagine a scenario in which you don't get to collect Santa-size satchels of taxpayer cashola.

OFFICIAL WHITE HOUSE INC. HOLIDAYS

January
- New Year's Day
- Super Bowl Sunday

February
- Reagan/Bush Day (formerly Presidents' Day)

March
- Negro Tolerance Day

April
- The Resurrection of Our Lord Jesus

May
- Dead Grunts Who Couldn't Score a National Guard Gig Day (formerly Memorial Day)

June
- Feast of the Divine Gerrymander

July
- Only Two More Days Until Our CEO's Birthday Day (formerly Fourth of July)

August
- Crawford Siesta Month

September
- Working-Class Pawn Day (formerly Labor Day)

October
- Joe McCarthy Day

November
- Pilgrim Witch Burning and Injun Rebuking Day

December
- The Birth of Our Lord Jesus

DRESS CODE AND GROOMING

Prelude: Understanding the Mandatory American Flag Lapel-Pin Policy

Flag pin with embedded spy cam.

Hand-forged by Texas campaign artisans from semiprecious metals and replica gemstones to accurately reflect our party's Godly monopoly on patriotism, the "Go USA #1 Flag" is every Bush staffer's single most important fashion accessory. Indeed, just as a puritanically plain Christian wedding ring serves to broadcast one's status as normal, this handsome, eye-catching lapel pin—when conspicuously brandished in accordance with White House Inc. protocol (left lapel, visible at all times)—identifies you as bona fide über-patriot and proud practitioner of opponent-stifling jingoism.

You must acquire your official American flag lapel pin with embedded spy cam from the employee commissary ($4,500) within twenty-four hours of commencing work at White House Inc.

Dominant Gender Dress Code

Appropriate Business Attire: When it comes to picking work-appropriate suits and shoes, simply invert the rule you traditionally apply to boys who wish to date your daughter: *the darker, the better.* Inasmuch as the GOP prides itself on being very inclusive, the entire color spectrum (from midnight blue to dark charcoal) of suits is welcome here at White House Inc. Be reminded, however, that while the GOP may be a big tent, it is not a circus tent. Stripes, paisleys, and other indicia of a weakness for style—long associated with the French, George Will, and other limp-wristed sissies—are not welcome.

Sports Coats: An ability to mix slacks and jackets smacks of an alarming predisposition to bipartisanship. If you insist on dressing like a Century 21 Realtor or NFL announcer, and still desire to be employed by White House Inc., please request Form 1903 ["I Want to Assist During Diplomatic Dinners"] and submit the completed paperwork to either catering or valet-parking services.

Undergarments: Your choice of masculine support is, of course, between your legs and the Lord. Be advised, however, that the full-body holographic scanners used at all entrances are sufficiently intrusive to detect any Lycra-blend bikini brièfs or any of the various other banana hammocks preferred by international terrorists and domestic homos.

Keeping a change of athletic socks stuffed into your BVDs may work well in filling out a Navy flight suit, but it can ruin the line on a pair of flat-front wool Dockers and lead to way more calls from Log Cabin Republicans than you can possibly return!

As generous contributors to the Administration, members of the Church of Latter-day Saints are exempt from such scrutiny. As such, each Mormon employee and all of his wives are encouraged to fill out Form 1119 ["I Wear Ridiculous Underwear and Only Take Them Off Weekly to Bathe Because I Belong to an Exotic Religious Cult."]

Hair Color: In light of the President's unfortunate use of Nice 'n Easy's Midnight Blue permanent hair color in the bathroom of Air Force One on the way to the 2003 G8 summit, all male staffers are now required to schedule *professional* rinses with a company-certified barber. Just ask for a "Gipper."

After-Work Fashion: The mandate for staid dress while in the White House does not mean you can't play dress-up when you leave the building. On the contrary, employment at White House Inc. affords every rich, well-connected American boy an opportunity to act out his pre–prep school fantasy of having a ruggedly virile occupation that requires him to don uniforms that are popular at after-hours Village People theme parties.

☆ **Remember: A 686 Silver Combat Magnum goes with anything, even those cheap Men's Wearhouse suits that Democratic senators and the boys in the kitchen wear.**

PICK A COSTUME AND MAKE IT YOURS:

☞ Cowboy (taken)

☞ Policeman

☞ Motorcycle Leather Fetishist

☞ Naval Fighter Pilot (taken)

☞ Fireman

☞ Catholic Priest

☞ Astronaut

☞ Crazed Mastermind Hiding in an Undisclosed Bunker (taken)

A convincing facsimile of regular cow folk.

A Note on Cowboy Verisimilitude: An old Texas saying about posers who pretend to be cowboys goes like this: "All hat and no cattle." Does this mean a rich New England populist wannabe shouldn't wear a cowboy hat? Certainly not! It just means a savvy would-be buckaroo should accessorize his crisp new Stetson with some genuine, rented long-horns. For example, if you are a Connecticut WASP set on running for President as the Lone Ranger, complete your broncobuster look by using money gained from family influence to purchase a Hollywood-quality Western ranch set in, say, Crawford, Texas. Then, when appearing on camera in your rootin'-tootin' hat on your new make-believe homestead, clear-cut enough brush to look as if you are preparing for the construction of an interstate cloverleaf exchange.

Gentler Gender Dress Code

Outerwear: In determining whether your attire is sufficiently feminine to pass the guidelines established by the enforcement arm of the Office of Gender Distinctions, allow former White House Inc. employee Karen Hughes to be your guide. If you persist on dressing like Bea Arthur, you will be packing your XXL cross-dresser power muumuus and sensible shoes for a flight out of our nation's capital before the next insider-stock-tip exchange shooter party.

Footwear: Focus on Heel Height: Next to choosing a personal savior, picking a pump altitude is the most important decision a GOP gal can make. You would, therefore, be prudent to exercise your unfettered freedom to settle on a heel size within the following guidelines:

Too Low: As the complimentary plastic tortoiseshell shoehorn you received in your new employee welcome packet states: "The sensible eschew sensible a shoe." A heel that doesn't make a percussive sound like a rusty Chinese pellet gun on a hardwood floor suggests a suspicious aversion to traditional feminine fashion martyrdom, which is all too often embraced by gals that attend all-female, nude, folk music and empowerment-poetry festivals and willfully spell "women" with a nefarious *y.* You know who you are—and so will we.

> *There is no doubt that a ripe, succulent bosom is an indispensable tool in luring a well-connected man into a lucrative Christian marriage. But once they have run a winning race, find a well-engineered bra and put those ponies in a saddle, gals.*

Too High: Heel height + your height > the President's height (accounting for hair-care products).

☆ **TIP: Avoid Shoes That Invite Intimate Groping: Strappy sandals or shoes that otherwise lewdly flash flesh below the ankles are only worn by harlots looking for trouble!**

Undergarments: While the Lord made the mistake of launching mankind in a makeshift nudist colony called "Eden," at White House Inc. you are expected to wear gender-appropriate, white L.L. Bean undergarments with the crotch panel intact. Also, your bra should be of sufficient tensile strength to keep you from spilling out onto your keyboard or into your hot coffee when not unhooked by a superior.

The Lord's Fashion Don'ts

As a Christian, you are required to strictly obey the Lord's inerrant tips on which female fashion accessories work best with an outfit. The Lord, speaking as He was wont to do—through apostle and fashionista Paul—is rather specific in this regard:

> "I also want women to dress modestly, with decency and propriety, not with braided hair or gold or pearls or expensive clothes."—1 Timothy 2:9

This means, of course, that Republican ladies must never wear gold, pearls, or anything from Neiman Marcus. If, however, you feel that such articles of clothing are "musts" or that expensive Italian clothing is the only thing that will work with your shoes, you must undertake the simple exercise that your CEO's mother (and all American Christians) routinely perform when faced with a Scripture that is either annoying or inconvenient: Ignore it!

A Note to Lady Staffers from Homeland Security

Entering the Building: At the First Lady's request, all female employees born after 1970 must have their panties and bras tagged by security each morning. With the help of a database developed by the Audubon Society, the First Lady will be able to trace any stray undergarments left under desks or dangling from doorknobs and personally return the lost items to their forgetful owners.

Leaving the Building: Black-light wands will be waved over your garments as you make egress from designated female exits. No woman will be permitted to leave the premises with any suspicious stains on her clothing, lips, or shoes. Please make use of our in-house, dry-cleaning service, which prides itself on reasonable prices, courteous service, and guaranteed DNA removal.

TEAM SPIRIT

While you're here to do a job for our military-industrial puppet masters, it's also a well-known fact that all work and no regimented play makes Jack a flabby nonteam player who might be susceptible to dangerous outside ideological influences. That's why the Human Resources Department has organized various fun activities to foster a robust facsimile of team spirit. Because without team spirit, we can't win—and if we can't win, then America is doomed to be run by effete, weak-kneed atheists willing to look the other way when marauding throngs of ghetto hoodlums ransack our coastal mansions and fence our mother's monogrammed silver flatware to be held over lighters by freebasing gangsta rappers.

ⓘ MANDATORY EVENT SCHEDULE

Mondays: Rooftop High Ropes Policy Synergy Session: Build trust and camaraderie as you scale a rope ladder to the summit of the antiaircraft turret and read aloud from autographed copies of *The Starr Report*.

Tuesdays: Creative Accounting Scavenger Hunt: Learn out-of-the-box thinking and unleash your inner solution finder in these weekly quests to conjure up evidence supporting Supply-Side Economic Theory.

Wednesdays: Ultimate Beast Wars: Relax watching anything-goes South Lawn interspecies death matches between champion Mexican cockfighters, rabid ASPCA strays, and fork-tongued adultery sleuth Linda Tripp!

Thursdays: Congressional Inquiry Thwarting Relays: Bone up on team problem-solving and testimony-corroboration skills with high-energy sprint relays between the Oval Office and subbasement document furnace.

Fridays: Military Fridays: Casual-schmasual! Arrive bedecked in authentic-looking combat camouflage fatigues purchased off eBay, and join our CEO in pretending to be in the military—with all of the pomp and none of the danger of getting within 5,000 miles of the enemy!

Saturdays: Wellness and Burnout Prevention Gathering: Foster people skills and explore new paradigms in sycophancy at this half-day indoor clay-pigeon shooting and individuality surrendering marathon.

Sundays: "Born-Again Birthday Bash:" Weekly after-lunch funnel cake and ceremonial garden-hose baptism parties to celebrate the anniversary of select employees' salvation from the fires of eternal Hell.

☆ OFFICIAL ☆ COMPANY CHEER!

Hey this is White House Inc. and we gotta say . . .
We're the monster mack–daddy who's here to stay!
(Clap)
So shout it loud, to anyone who'll listen . . .
We're kicking major ass on our military missions!
(Leg Kick)
Slashing taxes, drop-kicking the poor . . .
We may have it all, but we're gonna take more!
(Hands on Hips + Fanny Shake)
Money, power, eternal salvation . . .
Why deprive yourself when you own the nation?
(Cartwheel + Triple Hair Flip)
A few years from now we'll be sitting pretty . . .
Slurping tasty nectar from the corporate titty!
(Full Split)
So to anyone wondering who'll win the class war . . .
It's the same righteous posse that buggered Al Gore!
(Victory Shrieks + Jumping Pom-Pom Frenzy)

Dudes and Dudettes! Speaking as a former cheerleader—but not in a faggy way or anything—I know nothing stokes up ultra-major team spirit quite like having your very own custom cheer! Try this one out at the next company empire-building pep rally. I wrote it myself!

YOUR WORK AREA

In an effort to ensure that all staffers are protected from exposure to the soft-on-labor liberal theory of ergonomics, each workstation has been thoughtfully outfitted with wooden furniture designed in the Texas schoolhouse tradition. Along with a Stetson rack and handgun locker, your cubicle also comes fully equipped with a handsome lacquered pine plaque upon which Mrs. Bush used a blunt wood burner to lovingly scratch the words "God Loves You." (Depending on the time of day your particular plaque was completed, the inscription may trail off after the "God" part.)

Tired of that dowdy Nixon-era desk? Crafts to the rescue! Just dress up the sides with a smart decoupage made from used liquor-bottle labels!

Should you desire to make your workspace more unique, you may select an item from the list below.

Human Resources–Approved Decorations:

1. Limited-Edition, Framed Jigsaw Puzzle (to be hung forty-eight inches from the floorboard, immediately behind your desk): An ash-blond Jesus at the controls of a B-1 bomber giving the thumbs-up after decimating a whole village of unsaved peasants unfriendly to American petrochemical foreign policy (available in Persian, Oriental, or African villager styles).

2. A Lucite-encased passage from Mrs. Cheney's lusty, lesbian-erotica novel *Sisters* (Signet, 1981). Available for $50 (cash only) direct from the Second Lady, this sturdy tchotchke makes a wonderful paperweight or doorstop, and never fails to inspire with its warm, stirring excerpt:

> Let us go away together, away from the anger and imperatives of men. There will be only the two of us, and we shall linger through long afternoons of sweet retirement. In the evenings I shall read to you while you work your cross-stitch in the firelight. And then we shall go to bed, our bed, my dearest girl.
> —*Sapphic love letter written by Mrs. Richard ("Lynne") Cheney for her book* Sisters, *which many have argued is a coy, historical novel about famous American cross-stitcher— and cross-dresser—Betsy Ross.*

3. Motivating statuettes from Series Four of the "Greatest Dead Americans" bobblehead collection, currently commemorating six of our nation's most noble heroes: John Wayne, Richard Nixon, Sam Walton, Strom Thurmond, Jefferson Davis, and Lee Harvey Oswald. You may display a maximum of two (2) statuettes, lest your desk shudder too distractingly from the sheer patriotic might of their bobbling.

☆ **PLEASE NOTE: Workspace decoration is permitted not to indulge any inexplicable need to feign "personality," but instead to facilitate easy identification of your desk should Security need to hastily dispatch you into the trunk of an idling black sedan.**

Prayer Shrines

In collaboration with the Presidential Prayer Squad and corporate sponsors, larger offices are outfitted with collapsible prayer shrines made of sturdy laminated cardboard. Each prayer shrine features a watercolor of President Bush kneeling in the snow at Valley Forge, surrounded by a fluttering canopy of buxom angels and a picturesque forest of felled cherry trees. This stirring reproduction is ethereally lit with one forty-watt bulb (not included). Employees are directed NOT to substitute a higher-wattage bulb after the fire in Eunice Burn's office, which was caused by her mistakenly thinking she was witnessing a miracle for three crucial minutes of flames before calling Security. The public-address system will give you a five-minute warning before praying is to commence in earnest. You will also be given hints about what political victory or PlayStation disk the President needs.

THE MESS HALL

White House Inc. accepts the reality that it is occasionally necessary for workers to discontinue working long enough to consume the sustenance that powers their triple-overtime shifts. As such, the White House mess provides tasty and nutritious meals—all specifically chosen by President and Mrs. Bush.

MAIN MESS HALL: WEEKLY HOT LUNCH MENU

Sunday:
All-You-Can-Eat After-Church Buffet Featuring
- Salvation Salisbury Steak
- Lord's Own Liver and Onions
- Hot & Spicy Pentecostal Tongues

Vegetarian Option: Water Soup

Dessert
- ~~Devil's~~ *Angel* Food Cake
- Jesus Junket

Monday: (USA Day)
Main Dishes
- Creamed Eagle Gizzards on Wagon-Wheel Noodles
- Patriot's ~~Frankfurter~~ *Freedom Meat Pickles* Casserole
- American Cheese on Wonder Bread Sandwich

Vegetarian Option: Ketchup

Dessert
- Star-Spangled Jell-O Mold
- ~~Yankee~~ *Dixie* Doodle Sundae

I've personally tested this entire menu to ensure that nothing will stain your Tupperware with overly robust foreign sauces!

Tuesday: (Texas Day)

Main Dishes

- Broiled Squirrel in Mother Welch's Knorr Demi-glace Gravy
- Justice Thomas's Coca-Cola Hoppin' John
- Deep-Fried Possum Fritters with Sam Houston Jelly

Vegetarian Option: N/A

Dessert

- Moon Pie Flambé
- Peanut Butter–Stuffed Sow's Ears

Wednesday: (Tex-Mex Day)

Main Dishes

- President's Own Super-Carne Mexcellente
- Armadillo Chalupas
- Prairie Dog Tomatillos

Vegetarian Option: Rio Grande Smoothies

Dessert

- First Lady's Famous Jose Cuervo Sorbet

Thursday: (International Day)

Main Dishes

- Polish Sausage
- ~~Canadian~~ *51st State* Bacon
- Queen's Kidney Bangers on English Muffin

Vegetarian Option: Tossed Antarctican Field Greens

Dessert

- ~~Russian~~ *Soviets-Parading-As-Allies* Tea Cakes

Friday: (Pizza Day)

Main Dishes

- Beef Lover's Stuffed Pizza
- Pepperoni Lover's Stuffed Pizza
- Sausage Lover's Double-Stuffed Pizza

Vegetarian Option: Simply use fingers to extract meat from center of slice(s), please.

Dessert

- Hershey Choco-Pizza Nibblers

Saturday: (Picnic Day)

Main Dishes

- Hamburgers
- Corn Dogs
- Spit-Roast Your Own Fetal Pig

Vegetarian Option: Iceberg Lettuce Surprise!

Sides: (Special Mayonnaise-Based Salad Bar)

- Billy Graham's Miracle Whip Macaroni Salad
- Grandpa Prescott's Bavarian Potato Salad
- Jennifer Fitzgerald's Hot Tuna Salad
- Mother Bar's Chicken Neck Salad

Dessert

- Microwave S'mores
- Jenna's Magic Ecstasy Tart

Mess Hall Rules

1. No running, yelling, or roughhousing. Sole exceptions: anthrax evacuations, 2 Minutes Hate, and birthday gang-wedgies, respectively.

2. As robust Americans, we don't "queue" like the prissy English; we stand in line. Find the line designated for your rank, gender, and complexion, and wait patiently while your betters get a crack at the food while it is still warm.

3. Ensure that kitchen workers and helpers treat you with respect. Report any discourteous language (including Ebonics), resentful glances, or mysterious, squirrelly black hairs in your food to the food-service disciplinary manager immediately.

4. All persons must demonstrate proper Southern manners:

    a. Closed mouth while chewing anything other than tobacco

    b. Bibs for ribs

    c. Decorously hushed plotting only

    d. Fellas, your loafer/cowboy boot soles are to be flat on the floor at all times, and ladies, please, remember to keep your legs crossed at the ankles with your knees tightly together when not actually walking

    e. Expectoration in designated Loogie Hocking Areas only

A NOTE ON MESS HALL GUESTS

Legislative Branch: Capitol Building meal credits are NO LONGER ACCEPTED at the White House mess. Guests from the House and Senate must be accompanied at all times and may only enter White House dining facilities provided they (a) pay cash for hot lunch or (b) pack their own congressional slop.

Judicial Branch: As part of the December 11, 2000, agreement between James Baker and party loyalists in the Supreme Court, unlimited meal credits are provided in perpetuity for all justices whose framed photographs on the wall behind the chili cart don't have their teeth blacked out or derisive annotations scrawled across their faces.

5. Attempts by new employees to break into the Foreign Policy Team "cool table" rather than dining with Colin Powell are not permitted.

6. If a server continues to pour Coffee-Mate® nondairy creamer into your hot beverage after you have said "when," give the contents of your cup back to the insubordinate woman with a swift, lateral swing.

7. All midnight Skull & Bones tabletop sacrifices must be scheduled at least forty-eight hours in advance so that the chef can locate a defect-free female goat and have her FedExed in time for ritual deflowering and dismemberment.

8. The offering of gratuities to mess hall attendants is STRICTLY PROHIBITED. Studies have shown that tips only encourage third-generation, ethnic, minimum-wage high-school dropouts to become overly familiar and return your generosity by using the dollar to go on a malt-liquor binge, rendering them unfit to serve you the following day.

~~RECYCLING~~ *TRASH/DUMPING* **POLICY:** Please dispose of all bottles, cans, and newspapers in the ~~recycling bins~~ *garbage cans* located in the northeast corner of the mess hall. If the garbage cans are full, feel free to throw any refuse from your car window once you exit the compound at the end of the day. People are paid to clean up our city, let's help them earn a living!

RESTROOMS

Restrooms are provided without charge for your hygienic and excretory needs, and are located in several locations throughout the White House Inc. headquarters. For the sake of all employees, please take note of the simple guidelines below; careful adherence will ensure that punitive, lavatory shutterings remain at a minimum.

Everyone

1. No Smoking: In the wake of the unpublicized deaths arising from the 2001 Harvey Pitt methane fireball tragedy, smoking is now prohibited in all restrooms. Please feel free to exercise your right to enjoy non-addictive, noncarcinogenic tobacco products elsewhere in the White House compound.

2. Flush at Will: Be advised that the Clintonian "if it's yellow, let it mellow" water-conservation philosophy has been officially declared null and void. As such, the new (mandatory) White House flushing schema is as follows:

   a. Flush once to prime the toilet unit for waste acceptance

   b. Flush again immediately upon commencing release of waste product (to conceal unpleasant tinkle and/or plop sounds)

   c. Flush twice upon concluding business, once as a courtesy flush to expel waste from toilet unit, and once more to express contempt for endangered aquatic species

   d. If "Pinching a Hillary," execute repeated flushes as needed to dissolve any tenacious streak marks from porcelain

   e. During any visual inspection of your waste, it is preferable that you not verbally characterize what you see, cheer, or make other comments that may be upsetting to the person in the next stall (e.g., Mrs. Cheney's signature "When the Hell did I eat corn?" ruminations)

3. "Spare the Paper Towels, Spoil the Pacific Northwest Logging Economy!" You are encouraged to use a minimum of four paper towels per hand per washing. Remember, unless you're some tree-hugging enviro-mental, hand dryers are just there for dissipating fart fumes.

Women

1. **Minimize Primping:** The sinks are for washing filth off your hands, not for coloring your hair. If excessive time spent lavishing attention on hair, makeup, and pubic topiary designs is witnessed on the security monitors by Officer Johnson and his staff, these wholly frivolous moments will be tabulated by your unit manager and deducted from your pay.

2. **Injury Prevention:** Avoid sensible shoes with smooth or leather soles, as you will require the no-slip security of a rubber tread when hovering with your rear end precariously cantilevered over the opening so that you may go about your vile business without actually coming into contact with the germ-riddled seat—or, worse, one still warm from someone else's tushie.

3. **Pro-Life Procedures:** On-site monthly sanitary napkin funeral services may be held in the East Wing menstrual lodge.

Men

1. **Urinal Etiquette:** "Eyes on Thine Own Prize!"—do not (even accidentally on purpose) steal glances at the package of a neighboring colleague. Should you yourself experience a restroom encounter that is in violation of the President's "Don't Ask, Don't Ogle" Penis Peeker Policy, please report it immediately. Entreaties to enter a vacant stall for closer examination should, of course, be neither offered nor accepted.

2. **Shake It Out and Fly Right:** When conducting your post-urination jiggle, please take care not to dribble or splatter on the cowboy boots of your neighbor or yourself as calfskin is especially susceptible to unsightly urea staining. Ideally, you should use a single square of toilet tissue to gently dab the last remnants of pee from the tip of Acorn Andy's head. And remember to "zip up your zipper, don't let out the dripper!"

PARKING LOT

The White House parking lot is located between the West Wing and the Eisenhower Executive Office Building. It contains more than enough spaces to accommodate all of our employees' many SUVs, pickups, and Winnebago homes. Comprising nearly two acres of glistening, ecologically nurturing Kentucky blacktop, the lot is subdivided into two sections—each of which is monitored by 24/7 video surveillance and hourly patrols by autonomous, artificially intelligent killbots.[2]

☆ **NOTE: Per President Bush's express instructions, White House Inc. has discontinued the liberal, quota-inspired policy of designating all the best spaces "Handicapped." The good Lord must have had an inspired reason to make it hard for those people to get around!**

Sublot A (Premium)

This section contains thirty-five spaces reserved exclusively for executives and VIPs. Five spaces are reserved for visiting petrochemical lobbyists and extended members of the Bush family. In addition, the following vehicles have reserved priority parking spaces:

- Marine One (two spaces)
- Presidential Super-Stretch White Limousine (with hot tub)
- Presidential Black Limousine (with neon under-lights and rooftop mechanical bull)
- Presidential Segway Scooter (space adjacent to Red Cross First-Aid Station)
- Vice Presidential Ambulance
- Lynne Cheney's Dodge Barracuda
- First Lady's Bulletproof Mary Kay Pink Cadillac Escalade
- Secret Service Lincoln Continental War Wagons 1–3
- Jenna's VW Microbus "Girls Gone Wild" Party Van

[2] Inasmuch as these units are not optically sophisticated, but do download the latest racial profiles each morning, only approach your vehicle while wearing high-yellow to Caucasian colors, lest you suddenly find your neck pinned under a 300-pound mechanical knee until the next business day.

☆ **NOTE: Consult the White House Inc. intranet for hourly updates on the list of countries whose citizens or public officials have criticized or questioned your CEO. If you have a car from a country listed, you will be given thirty (30) minutes to remove it from the company's parking lot. Failure to do so may result in the vehicle's being towed away and detonated at a secure, undisclosed location.**

Sublot B (Standard SUV)

While there are no assigned spaces in this section, all drivers are asked to self-police enforcement of the parking policy, which stipulates that all spaces commonly perceived desirable by virtue of proximity to shade, the main entrance, or the GM-sponsored "Smog Day Afternoon" Internal Combustion Engine Appreciation Tent, be reserved for domestically produced SUVs only. Furthermore, inasmuch as there is only room enough for one space for each employee, your vehicle must have a current Blue Book value in excess of $75,000 in order to park sideways across two spaces, thereby depriving someone else of parking.

Parking Tags

Official parking permit hangtags ($2,500/fiscal quarter) must be hung from your rearview mirror at all times. These are nontransferable. If you are uncertain as to which section you are assigned, please see your manager for your parking-space allotment number. Violation of parking protocols may result in the President Himself keying your vehicle or, time permitting, steamrolling it under the wheels of his personal monster Hummer, the U.S.S. *Destructosaurus*.

TELEPHONE USAGE

Your work area has been outfitted with a state-of-the-art telephone system. For internal calls, simply wait a moment for a dial tone, then tell the helpful lady who answers what number you are calling. To place an outside call, you must first acquire written verification from Mr. Rove that you have clearance and justification to speak with outsiders. To place a long-distance call, simply notify the operator in advance so that she can set her egg timer to accurately record the duration of your conversation.

It may be tempting, but never brag to your extended family about how my Leak Subcommittee is recording all of their calls and following them to Wal-Mart.

Don't Forget

1. Always speak in a clear and pleasant phone voice, and when answering your extension, greet your callers by saying, "White House Incorporated. [Insert Your Name Here] speaking. What is it that you can do for us?"

2. When talking on the phone, remember that you are acting as a mouthpiece for your CEO. As such, it is imperative that usage of multisyllabic vocabulary be kept to an absolute minimum.

3. Calls to GOP big spenders that begin with "Hello, friend" are personal calls, not campaign solicitations. Otherwise, they would, of course, be in violation of federal law.

4. Unbeknownst to most, the expression "Cleanliness is next to Godliness" also applies to the little pink "While You Were Out" memos left for you by secretaries and the operator. Be sure to promptly stick a Zippo under any and all messages immediately after reading them, lest they get swept up in the net of a prying congressional subpoena!

USEFUL PHONE NUMBERS QUICK LIST:

9—Main Switchboard, 101—Oval Office, 302—Front Gate, 305—East Wing Reception, 275—Document Furnace, 777—Franklin Graham, 402—NORAD, 426—Janitorial, 102—Narcotics Anonymous—Hooters Hot Wings Express Delivery

SAFETY AND SECURITY

Safety

The importance of one's personal safety is, of course, directly proportional to his proximity to the zenith of our company's flowchart. Nevertheless, even if your job here at White House Inc. is so menial and numbingly repetitive that the President routinely brags to your coworkers and spouse that He could train Barney to replace you (given a handful of Snausages), White House Inc. is committed to maintaining a safe and injury-free work environment. Why? Quite simply, it takes an annoyingly long time to ideologically condition even the most insignificant new employee. As such, it is in the company's interest to ensure that you can survive the week without being shot in the head, drowning in the White House pool, or getting trapped between Mrs. Bush and her Gilbert's vodka cabinet during the afternoon happy hour(s).

SAFETY FIRST!

☞ Report unsafe conditions to the Chief of Staff. These may include, but are not limited to, indoor crude-oil spills, splintered Skull & Bones indoctrination paddles, and obstruction of an emergency exit by twenty-five or more loitering televangelism lobbyists.

☞ Do not hydrate more than twice per day from any water fountain that has been designated as a dual-use spittoon or spent Skoal Bandit repository.

☞ Second Amendment Day is the first Tuesday of each month. Please limit playful volleys of copy pool gunfire with your coworkers to this day only.

If You Are Injured

- IMMEDIATELY click your "I've fallen, and I can't get up!" receiver to summon your supervisor, who will confirm that you have completed and turned in your Employee Waiver Agreement and are not now, nor will you be in the future, aware of how to reach any trial attorney.

- Report to the subbasement infirmary for your single complimentary aspirin and American flag Band-Aid, as needed. If your pain persists and/or autoamputation is required, flag down any member of the Bush family for a hip-flask shot of single-malt whiskey.

Security

White House Inc. does its best to provide as secure a workplace as is possible in a country filled to the brim with violently deranged conspiracy theorists with constitutionally guaranteed access to weapons of minor and medium destruction. Its security protocols can be distilled into three important questions: (1) How do I get into the office? (2) How do I log on to my computer so I can download porn? and (3) What is preventing anyone else from messing with my stuff? As the President likes to say, "It's all about locks, codes, and hungry Dobermans."

 Locking Up: The President is the only person with a key to lock the White House from the outside. This master key, which automatically locks all doors and windows, can also be activated from a powerful remote pad[3] attached to the President's key chain. When He presses the activation button, you will hear two electronic chirping noises before all locking mechanisms are engaged. If He is scheduled to leave the White House, make sure you are outside or you will be locked in until the President returns. Oftentimes, the President wakes up in the middle of the night and walks out the front door to do His business off the Truman Balcony. This is not your concern as the door is left open during these times and security is standing by to discreetly hose away any urine, shattered Budweiser longnecks, and/or vomit from the rosebushes below.

 Pass Codes: Each staff member is provided with a list of several dozen pass codes. These alphanumeric strings, each of which must be changed weekly, are unique to you, and you are expected to commit them to memory. Your personal pass codes grant access to the primary alarm system, your workstation computer, the secure White House intranet, your locker, the restrooms, the mess hall, approved secure breakout rooms, the parking lot, the on-site Bally Total Fitness center, and the Hall of Prayer Closets.

• • •

---

[3] NOTE: Sometimes the President inadvertently sits on the keypad while riding in His limousine, causing doors and windows throughout the building to swing wildly open and slam shut in a repetitive frenzy. If this occurs, please stand clear of all building openings until the President is driven out of range.

Pass codes must consist of fourteen (14) or more characters and contain both upper- and lowercase letters, as well as no fewer than four (4) numericdigits and special characters. They may not begin with a special character or numeric digit or end in a special character, uppercase letter, numeric digit, or a lowercase *w*. Pass codes cannot contain any words from a dictionary, letters from your name, or Arabic slang words that may be construed as bomb threats. If a random manager-conducted workstation search should unearth any of your passwords—whether current or expired—written down, it will be considered a security violation and you will be escorted to the debriefing room for your resignation exit interview. And while the President, Vice President, and select senior staffers are exempt from this policy, Corporate Security nevertheless strongly urges all persons to discontinue writing pass codes on the palms of their hands in ballpoint pen.

Dobermans: Where human security can't go, Dobermans take over. These beautiful but deadly attack canines patrol sensitive interior and exterior areas of the White House complex. It is important to note that these "dog zones" are not officially documented and may change at a moment's notice. Therefore, it is likely you will inadvertently stumble into one and find yourself cornered by a pack of purposely underfed, homo-carnivorous Dobermans. When this inevitably happens, DO NOT attempt to flee, lest you raise suspicion from rooftop security and be unceremoniously machine-gunned into a blizzard of Alpo. Instead, fall to the ground, assume a fetal position, and cover your neck with anything you don't mind losing so your throat isn't torn inside out and we have to pay the Mexican groundskeepers overtime to resod patches of blood-caked lawn. Whatever the outcome, your generous insurance package will see to your needs. (See "COBRA and You," "Why Prosthetics Are à la Carte" and/or "Funereal Benefits.")

Understanding the Invited-Guest Body-Cavity Search Policy: President Bush realizes that there are few things less comfortable than watching a burly security guard slide his entire lubricated forearm into the rectum of your stirrup-bound grandmother. Sadly, in the post-9/11 world we live in, no one—not even the President Himself—is above sacrificing a degree of so-called privacy in the interest of ensuring we all remain protected from imminent murder by sneaky terrorists. As such, the President himself sets a patriotic example twice each week by standing behind a one-way mirror and supervising 300-pound White House security patriarch Mr. Otis Washington as he bravely jimmies a wide-bore speculum inside each congressional Democrat invited for bipartisan brainstorming. By following policy thusly, your CEO helps keep your workplace and country safe from all manner of contraband, plastic explosives, and biotoxin-wielding BenWa balls.

To outsiders, our security protocols might seem "excessive"—but that's just a fancy word used by effeminate liberals who read books and have never had to reload a rifle while cowering behind a pickle barrel riddled with Injun arrows!

Care and Maintenance of Your New GPS-Enabled Subcutaneous Chip: You can now stop wondering what that little lump is on the back of your neck. At the outset of orientation day, you and your new coworkers were gently rendered without consciousness. (Remember the pitcher of breakfast margaritas the First Lady kindly brought into the room?) You were then taken to the Office of Homeland Security, where a tiny GPS-enabled chip was implanted deep within your centermost neck vertebra in an arguably painless procedure involving a cotton swab and a pneumatic nail gun. The lump may fester and weep for up to a week, and it's fine to scratch at it all you like. Going forward, this chip is used to continuously monitor the whereabouts of you and your fellow White House Inc. staff members. You appear as a little red blip on a digital map of the world that covers the entire wall of the Secure Staff Monitoring Center, located 400 feet below the surface of a Shoney's parking lot just outside Martinsburg, West Virginia. Care and maintenance of your GPS-enabled subcutaneous chip occurs automatically each month without your knowledge via 128-bit encrypted stealth connection to the Total Information Awareness mainframe.

☆ **NOTE: All staffers are advised to think twice before seeking surgical chip removal after leaving White House Inc. While there is a wonderfully encouraging 72 percent survival rate for device implantation, no one has yet to brag about a successful removal.**

Your Responsibility to Carry Concealed Weapons: As a paid employee of the Executive Branch of the United States government, it is not your responsibility to legislate the law, nor is it your responsibility to interpret the law. That is what President Bush is here to do. Your job is to arrive on the premises fully prepared and equipped to *execute* the law—and anyone violating it. Which is why you are REQUIRED to exercise your Second Amendment right each and every day. Yes, whether your personal concealed firepower can knock a soda can off a fence or an apartment building off a block, it is welcome here at White House Inc. We ask only that when stowing weapons near your groin, you exercise caution to maintain the appearance of packing heat, not wood.

A Note on Handgun Concealment for the Ladies: Since truly feminine women are adroit at dressing to reveal, rather than conceal, working a hidden weapon into an outfit can take some careful thought—and a roll of masking tape. To help you tap into your girlish figure's hidden holster potential, the First Lady gives "Accessorizing with Ammo" workshops on the first Monday of each month. From slipping a trendy snub-nose pistol under the elastic waistband of your support hose, to accommodating a sawed-off shotgun beneath a pleated chiffon cocktail dress, the First Lady's got great ideas for any gal who still isn't used to walking around with a spare TEC-9 clip nestled between her derriere cheeks. There is limited seating, and her workshops fill up quickly, so it is suggested that you reserve a place at least one week in advance.

SICK LEAVE

Your CEO understands that nonjoggers occasionally become ill. As such, full-time employees are eligible for up to three (3) full days of paid sick leave per year. Persons wishing to be excused from work due to illness must adhere to the guidelines below. Failure to do so may result in withheld salary, written reprimand, immediate dismissal, and/or your being hunted down by security and ending up the lead story on the local news.

1. During sick days, employees must remain sick. Be aware though that you remain on call at all times and may be required to report to work in case of national emergency or fire drills.
2. All sick-day requests must be submitted in writing no fewer than seventy-two (72) hours before the onset of illness. Please note that in order to thwart malingers, multiple manager-conducted physical exams may be required to verify your alleged malady.
3. When returning to work, please deposit your proof-of-illness stool sample in the resealable jumbo Shedd's Spread Country Crock tub located in the center cabinet of the Secret Service coffee nook.

EMERGENCY LEAVE

Under certain absolutely unbelievably extraordinarily rare circumstances, employees may be eligible for short- or long-term leaves of absence. Your manager may determine other reasons for emergency leave and may grant emergency leave without pay for those reasons.

1. Death/funeral* of a child, loved one, or purebred pet
2. Critical illness of a biological child, loved one, or thoroughbred racehorse in which you have a minimum 40 percent ownership stake
3. Imprisonment of a relative for insider trading if the cumulative face value of the underlying transaction exceeds $700,000
4. Rumored impending interview by an Independent Council (this leave shall be with pay and include a cost-of-living adjustment for each exotic location)

*One of more of the following forms of documentation must be provided to confirm status of deceased: obituary clipping (the *Wall Street Journal* or the *Washington Times* only), memorial prayer card, embalming fluid receipt, or finger intact past the second knuckle.

VACATIONS

Oval-Shaped Office Occupants: You are limited to four (4) months of vacation each year, not including half days necessitated by naps, backyard games of catch with coworkers, or sundry incapacitations. In times of national crisis, such as when intelligence alerts contain specific, deadly, and catastrophic terrorist threats, you may find it necessary to limit a given Texas vacation to a mere four (4) weeks. Any vacation that results in photographs that prove useful in future campaigns are considered "working vacations" and do not count against your four (4) months.

Non–Oval-Shaped Office Occupants: You are limited to two nonconsecutive days of vacation, the schedule(s) of your superior(s) permitting. Said vacation days must be requested and approved in writing by the second week of each new fiscal year. Unused vacation time may not be carried over. For a list of approved vacation spots, please visit the Human Resources office and ask for the brochure entitled "Epcot Center & the Obsolescence of International Tourism."

HARASSMENT AND DISCRIMINATION POLICIES

While White House Inc.'s core, conservative philosophy is at odds with the liberal myth of discrimination, today's prevailing culture of victimization has unfortunately produced myriad ill-advised laws mandating a company-wide policy prohibiting all forms of so-called harassment.

Harassment of WASP Males

 If the company is to be compelled to attempt to excise the 100 percent natural prejudices that the Good Lord saw fit to instill in us 6,000 years ago, then it will forge bravely ahead to tackle the most pervasive, insidious, yet still condoned form of discrimination in America: bias against WASP males.

Therefore, under White House Inc. regulations, any less-than-effusive remarks regarding Christian white male-ness, sarcastic requests for million-dollar loans, derision of arrhythmic dance steps, replies in an uppity tone of voice, and other verbal or physical conduct of an irreverent nature constitutes unlawful harassment when such conduct either (1) substantially challenges an individual's acceptance of God's Divine Plan for Humanity (sometimes referred to in foreign code as "the status quo") or (2) effectively induces the object of such shocking disrespect to question his sense of entitlement, thereby recklessly imperiling all that is sacred to him.

Any employee found to have engaged in such conduct, or who condones such conduct by subordinates (either through concurrence or failure to issue a strenuous rebuke), will be subject to appropriate disciplinary action up to and including termination and/or transfer to Trent Lott's office.

Harassment of Broads

Despite accepted conservative logic that the weaker sex is not suited for service outside the bed-room—let alone in the Cabinet Room—President Bush has been proactive in recruiting loads of "easy on the eyes" babes for many suitable positions beneath the glass ceiling. Of course, this should in no way be interpreted as a triumph of feminist, bull-dykey thinking or as being symptomatic of the irreversible erosion of old-boy exclusiveness by the prevailing ideologies of liberal, man-hating, Diane Feinstein clones.

Therefore, it is the policy of this White House to strictly prohibit the documentable harassment of broads—in any form—whether it involves written communication, spoken communication, bra snapping, titty twisting, or simulated cooter-rooting tongue flicking between two distended fingers when there is reasonable grounds for belief that such actions will be unwelcome by the subjected female—even when she is not on the rag. In other words, just keep the party polite, gentlemen. Any employee having permitted the accrual of evidence of said transgressions will be directed to forthwith refrain from any and all such future carelessness, as well as to refrain from conspicuous post-harassment high-fiving.

> *We must respect and humor our little lady colleagues during the "career gal" phase of their nubile youths. After all, they'll soon be knocked up by wealthy Aryan stallions, at which time they'll make like good Republican wives and give up all this silly "working equality" and "pretending to know what they're talking about" stuff.*

DID YOU KNOW? The company's Broad Discrimination Policy reverently builds upon the proud foundations of GOP gender activism laid during the Anita Hill and Paula Jones sexual harassment cases. In the former, a gratuitously eloquent and credentialed Negress academic was righteously crucified for her un-American volunteer testimony against an eminenty qualified deaf-mute Supreme Court appointee. In the latter, a towering pillar of *Penthouse* centerfold virtue was aided and abetted in her noble for-profit lawsuit against our despised political nemesis.

Harassment of Coloreds

With the exception of his visceral opposition to affirmative action (see p. 112), integrated capital-murder juries, and that Martin Lawrence King Day thing, President Bush has been consistent in demonstrating a commitment to being perceived as a devoted friend of the Negro—so long as they are not loitering within 500 yards of a working voting machine.

Today, coloreds have equal rights to enjoy congealed gravy and bad service at Woolworth lunch counters around the country, and our President cannot help but feel a deep respect for their many contributions to our professional sports and common street-whore industries. As such, he is determined to foster an environment at White House Inc. where every last do-rag wearing Welfare Queen and Baby Daddy can dream of following in the glorious footsteps of Bob Barr, Clarence Thomas, Condoleezza Rice, and Colin Powell—and renounce all that "but I like being black" nonsense and start acting like nice high-yellow folks.

To show support for all the Negroes running around our country, I brought my Hattie McDaniel porcelain cookie jar to Washington. Bushie loves picking up her little bandanna head, looking inside, and saying, "Gee, this here Negro's head is empty. What are the chances of that?" And we laugh till it hurts!

Therefore, it is strictly prohibited for any regular White House employee to discriminate against coloreds in a manner that is egregious to the point of being able to withstand the "preponderance of the evidence" burden of proof in a civil court. If you feel you have been discriminated against or harassed because of your excessive pigmentation, you should take a long, hard look at your aspirations for a career in government, then entertain the ramifications of reporting it.

Harassment of Fruits

President Bush reluctantly accepts that factors such as sexual orientation do not adversely affect one's ability to execute most of the routine, day-to-day tasks required of all players on Team White House. For instance, if you are placed in charge of floral centerpieces for formal dinners or helping the First Lady select draperies for the private residence, your ability to take it up the Hershey Highway may actually be a vocational benefit. As such, the President is very proud to have arrived at a policy that panders to the Christian Coalition's rabid hatred of homos, yet still allows select Hell-bound sodomites to carpool separately on our shared one-way highway to tax-free ultra-affluence.

Indeed, the President has made it abundantly clear that He has no problem with homosexuality, just with "homosexual acts." Some non-Republican fruits and lesby-friends view this stance as contradictory. They are mistaken. In the end, it's no different from such perfectly sensible positions as, "It's not the fish I hate, it's the swimming," or "We don't hate Muslims, just the practice of Islam." Sadly, most homos are too brain-damaged by rave techno and poppers to even see the forest for the clear-cut trees.

> *I value my relationship-by-proxy with Log Cabin Republicans. So long as those people are filled with enough self-loathing to keep working on and donating to Republican campaigns, I'll be happy to ignore their selfish, girly shrieking each time I take another step toward stuffing them back into the dress-filled closets they tap-danced out of.*

Furthermore, contrary to popular belief, President Bush's repeated opposition to the decriminalization of fag sex in His home state of Texas was not because He is beholden to right-wing religious men who have a monomaniac preoccupation with homosexuality, but because the President feels so compassionately toward nancy boys that He wanted to ensure the preservation of a secure environment in which their aberrant lifestyle choice could be preserved and nurtured—jail.

CONSENSUAL SEXUAL RELATIONS

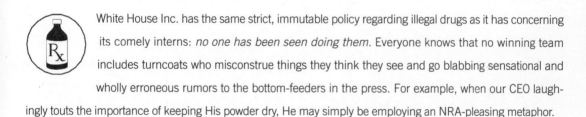

Whether you are a cabinet member who likes to bang secretaries in a leather sling, a deputy advisor who hungers for Travel Office trim, or even a speechwriting team that goes in for that sweaty man-on-man cornholing our Supreme Court seems so suspiciously crazy about, please remember that everyone is happily married at White House Inc. When it comes to sexual peccadilloes, as long as you can successfully fly under the radar of our more Puritanical supporters, no one at White House Inc. will piously smear your reputation with salacious details making future public-sector employment impossible. It is, however, your responsibility to ensure that all sexual indiscretions and other sins are conducted with a level of discretion that allows your coworkers to avail themselves to plausible deniability on the Sunday-morning talk shows.

ALCOHOL AND DRUGS

White House Inc. has the same strict, immutable policy regarding illegal drugs as it has concerning its comely interns: *no one has been seen doing them.* Everyone knows that no winning team includes turncoats who misconstrue things they think they see and go blabbing sensational and wholly erroneous rumors to the bottom-feeders in the press. For example, when our CEO laughingly touts the importance of keeping His powder dry, He may simply be employing an NRA-pleasing metaphor.

Bear in mind that neither the President nor the First Lady drinks alcohol, tells off-color jokes, or is addicted to menthol cigarettes. If, for any reason, you think you have witnessed anything that causes you to think otherwise, you are mistaken. Please commit this to memory if you don't wish to turn on your television and find yourself being diagnosed as a paranoid-delusional by a team of experts on *The O'Reilly Factor.*

All White House Inc. employees—other than the First Couple, of course—are encouraged to enjoy the stimulating and depressing roller-coaster effects of the buffet of mood-altering legal drugs traditionally favored by self-medicating Republican baby boomers. Approved substances to get your party going include nicotine, Valium, Xanax, Ritalin, caffeine, Paxil, alcohol, and whatever else you may find in the Betty Ford Apothecary Nook. Of course, the use of any narcotic more commonly associated with youthful Democrats or the cast of *Diff'rent Strokes,* however, is prohibited—unless your office is somewhat egg shaped and you are simply motivated to indulge by the gentle tug of nostalgia, not the ferocious grip of addiction.

ETHICS

WWBD? (What Wouldn't Bush Do?)

Let Faith-Based Ethics Be Your Guide

As an employee of White House Inc., you are expected to follow in the footsteps of our pious CEO. Your President applies the Lord's strict code of conduct to all business and personal matters, whether it's deciding which press corps reporters get "death stares" or which countries' leaders it's time to smite. In turn, when you are confronted with a serious matter that affects your conscience and challenges your personal integrity, you need only ask yourself the question, "What Wouldn't Bush Do?"—because you know that in following your President's example, you will also be emulating Jesus.

Regardless of what the hippy, Oprah Winfrey "Jesus Is Love" Christians try to tell you, the Lord Jesus was no pussy—flowing tresses notwithstanding. If you are in doubt of Jesus' ferocity, simply familiarize yourself with Matthew 13:41–42.

> The Son of man shall send forth his angels, and they shall gather out of his kingdom all things that offend, and them which do iniquity; And shall cast them into a furnace of fire: there shall be wailing and gnashing of teeth.

So in the hugely unlikely event your conscience should become troubled knowing your job is semidirectly responsible for high-casualty carpet bombings of Arabiac peasant villages, find comfort in knowing there is nothing we are doing that Jesus wouldn't do—only with more firepower!

PATRIOTISM

Someone famous once said that patriotism is the first refuge of scoundrels. That is exactly why this administration believes so strongly that you can never have enough scoundrels!

On October 26, 2001, President Bush signed the USA Patriot Act (USAPA) into law, granting White House Inc. sweeping authority over domestic law-enforcement agencies and international intelligence agencies. Our CEO has long held the sage belief that "there ought to be limits to freedom." And now there are. No more will we tolerate anti-American backtalk cleverly disguised as so-called free speech. The President would be the first to tell you (if He talked to anonymous drones in the hallways) that you are either with us or against us.

As such, patriotism will be enforced to the full letter of the law. As a White House Inc. employee, you are expected to demonstrate pure, unquestioning, and borderline lascivious adoration of the country at all times.

You will report any coworker we don't see through your U.S. flag lapel pin minicamera who engages in un-American behavior. This might be something as simple as patronizing a French bistro after work, or something more serious, like belonging to the ACLU, or tuning in to NPR for *Car Talk*.

Special rewards and incentives for turning in coworkers are available through the Reporting Internal Traitors Incentive Program. Frequent Informer points are redeemable in the Human Resources Department for a wide selection in jin-

"... and to the Republican Party, for which it stands. One nation, under me ..."

goistic, slogan-emblazoned jogging apparel and CDs of the hottest new country-and-western xenophobia ballads. Furthermore, please note that there is no need to brief your children on the rules for winning candy, PlayStations, and ponies for informing. They have already been told.

V.
DOMESTIC
POLICY

INTRODUCTION

In a Suit, Following Suit: The Importance of Staying "On-Script"

It is no coincidence that President Ronald "The Great Communicator" Reagan was for many years a beloved professional actor before heeding God's call to save the world. And while his dramatic talents may have never been formally recognized by the coastal intelligentsia, any member of his political entourage will readily attest to his brilliance at appearing affably semi-cognizant while reciting other peoples' words and ideas. Indeed, whether performing in such cinematic masterpieces as *Girls on Probation* (1938), delivering stirring ad copy as a chain-smoking pitchman for Chesterfield cigarettes, or gamely emoting his way through the giddy, communism-toppling speeches of former Hallmark ringer Peggy Noonan, the Gipper knew full well that improvising on a well-written script could ruin a shot quicker than a scene-stealing monkey.

As a wholly owned, carbon-based subsidiary of White House Inc., you are obligated to carefully emulate President Reagan in all regards (other than a tenacious control of your bowels at staff meetings). Of course, should your perfectly understandable hatred of everything about the liberal, faggy world of Hollywood make it difficult for you to cozy up to the notion of "scripts" and "acting," simply tap into America's rich heritage of evangelical Christianity, and read aloud from White House gospel with the same salesmanship and zeal that a millionaire televangelist summons to whip a revival tent full of unemployed textile-mill workers into signing away the deeds to their split-level ranch houses.

The following pages contain important domestic policy boilerplate for invocation during conversations with your like-minded friends and family, as well as handy debate facts for use in all heated, acrimonious shouting matches you may initiate with patchouli-dipped, bleeding heart, America-hating, spit-on-Christ Democrats.

Physical Fitness Through Owning Sports Teams

 Physical fitness is President Bush's signature domestic issue—more important than the homeland security reelection stuff, avenging paternal humiliations, and even petrochemical-lobbyist payback. A borderline professional runner, your CEO is a firm believer in looking supergood in those lined shorty-shorts that let your manhood swing like the tongue on the Liberty Bell. And inasmuch as He values a lifestyle of rigorous physical activity more highly than anything, our President cannot abide lard asses, spazoids, cripples, or little sissies anywhere within His administration and/or country.

> *Nothing whoops a Coors Light hangover— next to some hair of the dog, of course—quite like a good-morning uvula diddle followed by a stumbling, pain-is-purifying, toxin-sweating, seven-minute-mile jog.*

☆ **FUN FACT:**

As an accomplished athlete, the President loves to watch sports teams on TV almost as much as making sure-thing investments in them with His father's friends' money. His current favorite televised sport is "Run from My Laser-Guided JDAMs of Death You Worthless Arabiac Sand Monkeys."

That's why on June 20, 2002, George W. Bush signed Executive Order #13266, forming the President's Council on Physical Fitness and Sports. This body, composed of twenty appointees from the President's steroid-engorged Rolodex of locker-room towel snappers and flabby former Olympians, advises White House Inc. on policies to help keep wealthy white folks from drowning in gaping sinkholes of their own jiggling ass cellulite.

Your CEO is confident that, in the end, only the most beautiful, physically fit sycophants will be chosen to enter the Kingdom of the Righteous and commence repopulating the world—*correctly* this time. Of course, God didn't intentionally create the middle class, the colored, and lesbian semiotics professors at Brown University, but next time around, President Bush is determined to remedy the Almighty's egregious error. "After all," the President reminds staffers, "when the Lord said 'gluttony is a sin,' He was talking about doughnuts, not stock options."

☆STAFF NOTE: The corporate culture of White House Inc. is one of red-blooded, healthy devotion to the professional athleticism of other males and the statistics they create. The Company cannot be held liable for any mama's-boy brainiacs who get depantsed, purple nurpled, swirlied, or worse. Furthermore, all fatties are advised to adopt a strict regimen of chocolated laxatives, ephedrine, and participation in any or all of the following compulsory, strenuous, organized sports and activities:

- South Lawn Red-Tape Hurdles
- Group Bullworker Sculpting
- Female Bodybuilder Thunderdome with Don Rumsfeld
- Skull & Bones Gluteus Maximus Massage and Trust Circles
- Planned Parenthood Doctor Kickboxing
- Dick Cheney's Cardio-Blast Workshop
- XTREME Washboard Ab Sculpting with
  Mrs. George. H.W. ("Bar") Bush
- Step and Fetch Class w/ Condi and Colin

9/11 and How It Fits into Campaigns

Nature Abhors a Vacuum; When Buildings Fall, Popularity Rises!

The horrifying events of September 11, 2001, represented a distinct turning point in George W. Bush's tenure as our beloved CEO. Before that fateful morning, He was a Commander in Chief without a mandate, without the technical nicety of having been chosen by the voters, without a chance of ever having His southward-bound approval ratings ever rise back above 47 percent. But by 8:45 A.M. on Nine-Eleven™, the last of those things had changed, and our Supreme Commander took a swift, one-way detour off the "Bush I" expressway to early retirement.

Within hours, as He zigzagged His way around the country, proactively taking refuge under His Air Force One meal tray, President Bush's ratings skyrocketed nearly 45 percent, all the way to 90 percent approval—a level not seen since His father so wisely wrapped up Gulf War #1 instead of felling the conquered and helpless Saddam Hussein. Not surprisingly, our CEO's competency also doubled. His appreciation of international cultures increased by 45 percent, as did His mastery of global diplomacy and strategic Crusade references. Yes, so fundamentally transformed was our Leader that were He to have been transported back to His freshman year at Yale through a quantum rip in the space-time continuum—even His academic performance would be 45 percent better—perhaps as stratospheric as a B-minus average.

Suddenly, awkward pauses were moments of careful contemplation. Looks of detached disinterest were signs of calm resolve. Hostile glares at domestic reporters were the reassuring indicia of a steely determination to kill some foreign trash. In short, 9/11 transformed the President into 200 percent the man He was when He passed out the night before. The nation willed itself into having the President it needed. Like a collective hysterical pregnancy—only with real afterbirth. And it is this new, different President's solemn oath before Jesus that the people who perished in the World Trade Center towers will not have died in vain. Indeed, how light would be their collective hearts if they knew what a vital role their otherwise unfortunate demise will play in partisan television spots? It is, therefore, out of respect for their bravery that we employ the alchemy of politics to turn their tragedy into the type of star-spangled patriotic fervor that overlooks the ethics of Nixon and the economy of Hoover to fill convention halls with red, white, and blue balloons and crates of preprinted absentee ballots.

Campaign Tip:
Choose from these RNC-approved "wedge terms" when labeling leviers of any substantive criticism against White House Inc. policy.

- "Terrorist Coddler"
- "Traitor/America-Hater"
- "Radical Liberal Agenda Promoter"
- "Christ-Killer"
- "Dummycrat"
- "Homo-Loving, Welfare Stamp–Licking, Background Check–Worshipping, Carter-Fellating, Left-Wing Pussy"

Terrorism: Fomenting Constant Terror Thereof

 Before 9/11, America's liberal television news media subsisted on whatever meager, apathetic viewership it could muster through a tried-and-true formula of twenty-four-hour coverage of toddler-devouring sharks, Negro celebrity trials, and limitless Peabody-worthy reporting on the comings and goings of a certain former President's happy-go-lucky love muscle. But today, all those topics have been rendered worse ratings poison than Strom Thurmond's home porn, relegated to the sidelines by a revolutionary new White House–devised election-sweeps ratings jackpot: "All Terror, All the Time!"

There is nothing more compelling and exotic to a constituency than having their pants ooze with the malodorous emissions of hair-whitening fear. Living in abject terror is a grand tradition in societal pacification and domestic myopia, and as harbingers of the coming Republican nirvana, it is our duty to milk the sweet nectar of constantly simmering hysteria. As such, understand that it behooves every White House employee to invoke the ghastly, razor-fanged specter of terrorism no fewer than seventy-five times per day, with subtly oscillating degrees of panic.

In keeping with his personal philosophy of Compassionate Conservatism, President Bush is committed to selflessly helping Americans feel better about themselves and their circumstances by artfully employing the pleasantly distractive qualities of eternal paranoia. Dejected over long-term unemployment? Be thankful you haven't been disemboweled by a box cutter–wielding, Koran-babbling Arabiac! Uncertain how you'll survive retirement on a now-worthless 401(k)? At least your cul-de-sac hasn't been encircled by a bloodthirsty horde of explosives-laden, yelping Afghans and their foam-drooling, rabid camels!

☆**TIP: Assemble your own FEMA-compliant Terrorism Survival Kit: three days' supply of water (or other, more mature beverage), food, batteries, a portable radio, duct tape, plastic sheets, a chemical shower, a stockpile of 5,000 mg Cipro IV caplets, the complete books-on-tape New Testament as read by Charlton Heston, two chainsaws, an M-16, and your own personal Cayman Island.**

Terrorism Talking Tips

Should someone attempt to engage you in substantive policy debate not related to terrorism, rebuke them as follows:

Them: "I'm concerned that the gap between rich and poor is widening."

You: "So tell me, what does Osama bin Laden's dick taste like, you Arab-felching traitor?"

Them: "I support a woman's right to choose."

You: "If you hate America so much, why don't you go live in Muslamia? Faggot!"

Them: "How can we expect to pay for our own defense if we continue to slash taxes for the ultrawealthy?"

You: "What are you, a French pansy or something? Fucking liberal!" (Teeth-shattering-punch)

Common Questions About Terrorism

Q: Why did the freedom-hating cowards attack us?

A: Because they hate freedom, and they hate peace, and they hate free peacefulness. (Any deeper analysis of the motives behind an exponentially multiplying population of psycho-zealots shows suspicious equivocation and is pointless.)

Q: Isn't it true that former President Bill Clinton practically *begged* terrorists to kill us?

A: Yes. He *and* the entire America-hating cowards in the Democratic Party did. So strong was his repellant sympathy for those who burn the American flag, he used his engorged penis to hypnotize all the Republicans who controlled the House, Senate, Armed Services, and Intelligence Committees. Entranced thusly, they found themselves regrettably, yet out of acute political emergency, helplessly focusing on the presidential crotch rather than a bunch of mumbo-jumbo talking Islamiac loony birds who never even merited a single *National Enquirer* cover.

Q: How can we prevent terrorism?

A: The best way to prevent terrorism is for the obedient populace to be limber in their outrage, rapidly adapting their ire and flexibly screaming for the deaths of any new civilian population Condi pulls out of the

"Easy Enemy of the Month" hat. If folks stay busy shrilly denouncing the deprivation of foreign folk's rights, they are less likely to be needlessly troubled by the painless removal of their own liberties that have traditionally encumbered them here at home. Other than that, they can always visit Walt Disney World while it's still open.

Q: How long will the War on Terrorism last?
A: 127 years. Or longer.

Q: What are the best songs to embed in commemorative 9/11 PowerPoint montages?
A: Carl Orff's *Carmina Burana* and/or The Cure's "Killing an Arab."

Homeland Security

On October 8, 2001, President Bush signed Executive Order #13228, summarily jettisoning decades of Republican aversion to money-hemorrhaging big government and forming the all-new Office of Homeland Security. Elevated to a full-fledged, Cabinet-level department by Congress on November 19, 2002, Homeland Security accomplishes a major reorganizing of national skulking and disinformation by combining dozens of smaller, marginally effective bureaucracies into one gloriously obese, utterly sedentary bureaucracy, which itself remains totally dependent on information provided by the crackerjack preventative investigators of the FBI and CIA.

Upon ascending to Homeland Security from my previous lousy gig as governor of Amish-infested Pennsyltucky, I immediately set nose to grindstone, developing the categorically perfect, nonfrenzy-inducing Terror Code Alert System, which offers 100 percent protection against Arabiac first-class cabin kamikazes. Look for routine escalations of the alert level during all national holidays or whenever ruthlessly insidious foreign factions cause the President's approval rating to erode by 5 percent or more.

Beyond its secondary mandates to issue color-coded CYA alerts and ensure the smooth execution of vital Texas redistricting, the Department of Homeland Security is charged with four primary tasks:

1. Controlling our borders to prevent Mexicans, homo-marrying Canadiacs, medical marijuana, and thermonukular thingamajigs from entering our country.

2. Bringing together our most ineffectual Washington middle managers and cubicle trolls, who, like the President they so gloriously serve, were all so stunningly transmogrified by the events of 9/11 that they are now dedicated, supercompetent worker bees capable of generating three times their own considerable weight in paper between their many daily coffee and danish breaks.

3. Waking up otherwise sleepy state and other territorial local authorities by assuming rage-inducing, patronizing control over any and all investigations that strike their fancy.

4. Most important, composing classified memoranda about their preliminary reviews of the secret files whose contents might inform the creation of possible exploratory task forces for the potential establishment of procedures for hypothetically strategizing theories for thinking about avoiding danger and mass death.

In forming the Department of Homeland Security, this administration is communicating that its highest priority is to shield America's red-voting states from understanding the troubling roots of ballooning, global anti-Americanism. Because you never know where terror will strike, and that's why it's best just to assume that you personally are in imminent danger of having your face melted clean off your chattering skull by a nasty case of weaponized Nuke Pox. And if it doesn't happen, the warned possible victims are so relieved, they thank us instead of questioning our intelligence or motives. In other words, banging the drum of terror is a win-win for everyone!

☆ **HOMELAND SAFETY TIPS:**

Be vigilant! The enemy is all around. Staff members observing any of the following are hereby commanded to contact the FBI immediately:

☞ Brown-skinned persons conversing in heated jibberish.

☞ Facial hair on anyone other than Italian women.

☞ Turban-wearing persons demonstrating emotions other than all-American bliss and contentment.

☞ Sidewalk falafel vendors of ambiguous ethnicity who are unwilling to make change for a fifty.

☞ Arab store owners or cabdrivers who try to conceal their hatred of our country by prominently displaying more than three American flags.

☞ Middle Eastern persons who become visibly uncomfortable and/or upset when confronted with your constructively suspicious queries about their personal hygiene or why they worship Muhammad Ali.

☞ Burka-clad transvestites.

Understand the System

HOMELAND SECURITY ADVISORY SYSTEM

CHAOS
APOCALYPSE NOW UNFOLDING

PANIC
ARABIACS AT YOUR FRONT DOOR

PARANOIA
SUSTAIN. REELECT. REPEAT.

APATHY
STATUS QUO NAVEL GAZING

STUPOR
LIMBAUGH. FRIENDS. SURVIVOR.

RED
ORANGE
YELLOW
BLUE
GREEN

The Federal Budget

Key details of your CEO's inspired operating budget follow:

Department	What We Will Tell the Voters We Accomplish	% Change from Clinton Budgets
Dept. of Agriculture	Render the tractors, grain silos, and livestock insemination systems of America's agriculture conglomerates wholly impervious to sabotage by TERRORISTS.	−27.9% ↓
Dept. of Commerce	Sweeping initiatives to safeguard American bar-code scanners, cash registers, and Wal-Mart patio furniture inventories from the scourge of TERRORISTS.	−12.4% ↓
Dept. of Defense	Realize a breathtaking increase in contracts awarded to defense-industry facilities located in the home districts of congressional Republicans, thereby ensuring an ever-expanding nukular weapons stockpile for use in the never-ending war against toenail-clipper-wielding TERRORISTS.	+ 15,892% ↑
Dept. of Petroleum Protection	Write blank checks to cover contracts to companies connected with Dick Cheney or the Carlyle Group to rebuild what we just spent billions of dollars destroying in the Middle East—aka TERRORSTAN.	(new)
Dept. of Education	Protect America's parochial school students from the insidious dangers of TERRORISM, evolution mysticism, TERROR, affirmative action, secularism, and/or TERRORISTS.	−31% ↓
Dept. of Energy	Expand the capacity of U.S. petrochemical conglomerates and their stockholders to traffic in foreign oil without suffering reduced profits due to TERRORISM. Also, the occasional yanking of the Ace Hardware extension chords that hold our nation's 1950s energy grid together, as a reminder to everyone of how susceptible we all are to TERRORISM.	+47% ↑
Dept. of Faith	Aggressively liberate the imprisoned Christ-worshipper trapped within EVERY American and potential TERRORIST by overwhelming Protestant churches with even more cash than typically passes through their many tax-free bank accounts.	+11,983% ↑
Dept. of Health	Establish an impenetrably healthy buffer zone between Americans and TERRORISM in the form of heavily fortified insurance-company profit margins.	−31% ↓

Department	What We Will Tell the Voters We Accomplish	% Change from Clinton Budgets
Dept. of Homeland Security	To whip Americans into a state of frenzied hysteria through a scientifically precise series of increasingly shrill TERRORIST alarm colors so they are too afraid to travel, thereby doing away with the expense of protecting airports, aircraft, and Greyhound buses from TERRORISM (money that can be more productively given directly to Halliburton).	(new)
Dept. of Housing	Implementation of advanced video surveillance/facial recognition technologies throughout urban low-income housing—the traditional breeding grounds of TERRORISM.	–12% ⬇
Dept. of Interior	Proactively pursue the systematic deforestation of vast tracts of domestic woodland to thwart the camouflaging of potential Viet Cong–like TERRORISTS on our shores.	–17% ⬇
Dept. of Justice	Printing pamphlets to explain to arrested civilians that they have TERRORISTS to thank for the snatching away of several of their erstwhile popular constitutional rights, and the cracking down on smutty girl-on-girl videos favored by TERRORISTS and domestic EVIL DOERS.	+67% ⬆
Dept. of Transportation	Construction of 14-lane loop roads to alleviate the inconvenience of public transportation in Republican districts, coupled with exponential increases in roadside strip-searches of immigrants, leftists, cock-teases, and other TERRORISTS.	+3% ⬆
Dept. of Treasury	Completion of covert program using plastic "anticounterfeiting" global positioning tracking strips in U.S. currency to electronically monitor all cash transactions—the overwhelming majority of which are conducted by TERRORISTS posing as American civilians.	+71% ⬆
Dept. of Veterans Affairs	Teaching blue-collar suckers too old to fight TERRORISTS and too stupid to avoid war that if they wanted health care, they should have landed a choice post in the National Guard and then sponged off their parents' friends.	–83% ⬇
EPA	Providing bottles of white out for redaction of all references to "Global Warming," "Greenhouse Effect," and other TERRORIST code words from EPA documents. Also, relaxation of so-called pollution laws to ensure that our skies are rendered more opaque, making it impossible for TERRORISTS who have commandeered aircraft to see their targets on the ground.	–98% ⬇

Department	What We Will Tell the Voters We Accomplish	% Change from Clinton Budgets
Medicare/Medicaid	Ensure that wealthy senior citizens can continue to receive their expensive, life-extending medications without actually having to rub elbows with the rest of the dying population. Charge remaining senior citizens nominal charge for all the free aspirin trial packs they can gum before getting murdered by TERRORISTS.	–91% ↑
NASA	Realign America's space program away from girlish, disaster-prone science, and toward the rapid development of the super-smart orbiting ray beams and missile shooter-downers required to render us immune to TERRORISM.	–17% ↓
National Endowment for the Arts	Aggressively seek out America's overeducated, artistic elite, ask them to submit proposals for grants that can explore multiculturalism, political correctness, patriarchal power structures, the horror of war, and the smearing of genitals in chocolate syrup. Arrest applicants en masse, ship to Camp X-ray, and prosecute them as domestic TERRORISTS.	–97.8% ↓
National Science Foundation	Quantum microscopic leaps forward in the development of personal rocket packs, hydrogen-fueled SUVs, and the technological underpinnings of the super-cool Strategic Continental Cloaking Initiative—capable of making all of North America invisible to TERRORISTS.	–86% ↓
Small Business Administration	Continue convincing penny-ante entrepreneurs that they share the same tax burden as multibillion-dollar corporations, further obscuring the fact that Mom and Pop will eventually foot all tax bills while GOP CEO-buddies selflessly provide golf-caddy jobs to the same military reservists who keep us safe from TERRORISM.	–23% ↓
Social Security Administration	Sell to The Money Store, thereby successfully transforming Franklin Roosevelt's socialist abortion into a red-blooded pillar of privatization, reaffirming America's faith in the noncrooked stock market, and clearing the way to transform elder-care community centers into anti-TERRORISM Soylent Green factories.	N/A (0%)

The Economy

White House Inc.'s approach to the economy is called "Bushonomics." Study the informative chart below to arrive at a comprehensive understanding of this inspired economic model.

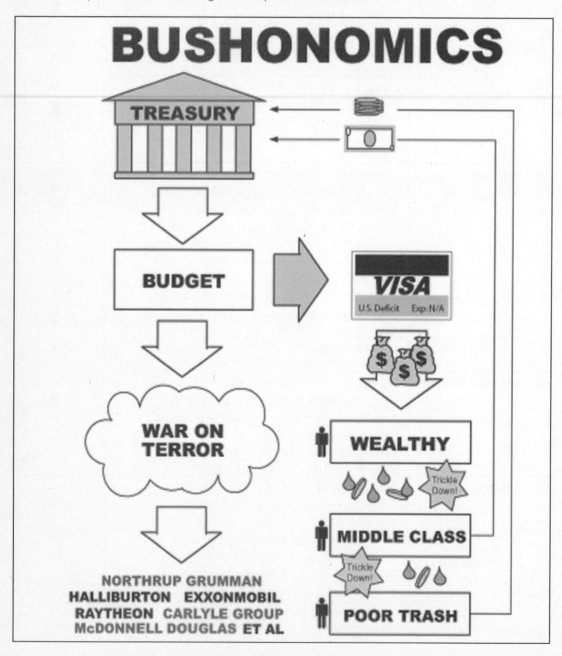

Capital Punishment

The President knows that prosecutorial misconduct is a liberal myth and that it's a statistical fact that killing crooks—especially uppity, insane folks and mongoloids—both reduces crime and keeps property values stable in the charming, gated neighborhoods that our most generous Corrections Industry supporters call home. That's why, of the countless great things President Bush did for the state of Texas, the one He is most proud of by far was presiding over a record 152 compassionate executions.[4]

On execution days, then-Governor Bush took great righteous pleasure in listening to His phone ring for hours on end, knowing it was some undereducated public defender wanting to cry about "planted evidence" and "forced confessions," then beg like a woman for a stay of execution until some science-fiction "DNA tests" could free their client to go out and start collecting welfare again. Sometimes, the governor couldn't help but pick up the phone and say, "Domino's Pizza. You just wasted your one call, sucker!" Other times, he would delight friends and coworkers gathered in his office with his famous Karla Faye Tucker imitation, blubbering to the dumbstruck lawyer: "This is Karla. Please don't call me. I'm busy burning in HELL!" On many such occasions, Mr. Bush would show so much statesmanlike poise, he managed to get through the entire call without bursting into knee-slapping guffaws.

In June 2002, the President was highly dismayed when the Supreme Court of the United States, in its candy-assed hand-wringing ruling in Atkins v. Virginia, declared the execution of retards to be unconstitutional. Unlike those dour legal types, the President knows from personal experience that most retarded people—in addition to being inexplicably sticky—are really just pretending. Besides, even if you have to kill five purportedly innocent retards to catch just one white-woman-molesting black man, that's a price most Americans are willing to pay.

☆ **DEATH PENALTY FUN FACTS:**

☞ The earliest historical record of crucifixion dates all the way back to 519 B.C.

☞ By late 2007, Texas will be the first state to resourcefully employ derelict, wooden utility poles (rendered otherwise useless by the burial of power and telephone cables) as decorative, roadside crucifixion devices for all death-row inmates.

☞ The President supports the expansion of the death penalty to such crimes as sedition, press leaks, dating outside one's tax bracket, and colluding to interfere with the power and prestige of the Electoral College.

---

[4] Not counting that Austin pedestrian who was taunting traffic in front of the governor's mansion on a rainy night in February 1998.

Energy and Power

 Americans are a people of hearty appetites. We hunger for heaping servings of everything to which we are so rightfully entitled: big cars, big homes, big landfills, and a limitless supply of Super-Maxi-Size Turbo-Extra-Value Meals. As such, our per capita energy consumption understandably eclipses that of all the other inferior nations with which we must temporarily share the planet. The President understands this and believes it is our duty as Americans to indiscriminately drill, invade, and/or kill as is needed to maintain the steady flow of energy required to ensure that none of us—income providing, of course—should ever experience the agonizing sting of non-instant gratification.

In all policy discussions relating to energy, this administration is of course referring explicitly to fossil and atomic fuels. Oil, coal, natural gas, and nukular plants are the only legitimate sources of power for true Americans— short of slavery. Sun, wind, hydrogen, vegetable oils, and ethanol reek too pungently of "save the world" hippy nonsense and Green Peace pirates to ever fall from the tongues of real Republican men. Of the "green" energy options, only wood-burning and hydro power plants have demonstrated any potential. The former, when thoughtfully established in locales where Lyme disease–harboring, old-growth timber needs eradicating, and the latter, only when a dam can strategically transform an entire Democratic voting district into a modern-day Atlantis.

Without energy, there would be no cars, and without those evergreen symbols of American freedom, there would be no car commercials bellowing in our living rooms, rousing our fellow citizens from their indolence into a credit-leveraging frenzy. And then we might as well all be living in eco-freako California or Red China, where grown, slanty-eyed man-dwarves too stupid to know they should covet Camaros blithely settle for teetering around on sissy bicycles.

Fortunately, the President has a clearly defined plan that gives emphatic lip service to energy efficiency, conservation, and the development of cleaner technologies while still guaranteeing plenty of major blackouts and maintaining His family's faithful and unimaginably profitable devotion to Arab oil.

Judicial Nominations

 White House Inc. is committed to appointing the wisest and most competent federal judges available from the rarified population of "strict constructionists." That is, people who hold dear the notion that our nation is frozen in 1787, when the ink on the Constitution was still wet and Americans were free to own slaves and treat their heart disease with a bottle of hungry leeches.

Your CEO seeks judges who are virulent abortion-haters, yet have had such unremarkable careers that they have left no written record of their opinions about abortion and are, therefore, credibly able to appear before a Senate panel and claim they are so vacuous when it comes to thoughts of morality and legality that they possess "no current opinion" on the obscure, esoteric topic of abortion. This ability to deftly slip under liberal radar is precisely why Concerned Women for America praised President George H.W. Bush for being resourceful enough to cleverly engineer Clarence Thomas's dramatic pole-vaulting into the U.S. Supreme Court directly from the D.C. traffic court across the street!

A successful nominee must also be able to provide White House Inc. with adequate judicial cover when long-overdue curtailments of luxuries, such as civil liberties like the mostly abused right to free speech, are swiftly enacted under the cover of whatever war our CEO happens to be conducting at the time. This administration's battalion of judges will also oversee compliance with established and emerging conservative laws and statues, such as parental notification for preggers, penis-addicted sluts, and the day-to-day erosion of the troublesome inconvenience of the constitutional preference for the separation of church from state.

Congressional Democrats like to complain about my "stealth nominees." Well, they said the same thing about David Souter back when my daddy found him holed up like the Unabomber in a filth-strewn New Hampshire cabin—and hell if he didn't turn out to be a squirrelly weasel shit-for-brains liberal!

~~Affirmative Action~~ *Equal Opportunity*

It doesn't matter if you are a crack baby who had to dodge bullets to get to a public school where teachers might not even show up to speak in Ebonics, or a proper gentleman raised by imported servants in a Tudor mansion—the President believes that everyone has a place in this world. Indeed, whether it is the indolence of a lifetime of service in the sanitation industry or the essential contributions made in the fast-paced life of a Wall Street broker, all American citizens have an equal opportunity to rise to their predestined potential.

As children of the same God, we understand that wherever He pops us into this world, we are placed there as part of His glorious and divine plan. So-called advancement is up to Him, and no matter how high up in the air God holds the hoop, either you jump through it or you don't. To question where you end up is to rebel against the living God and rudely question His judgment. The President calls it "rocking the boat," and, keeping with the metaphor, "affirmative action" is just a fancy phrase for "making waves." This administration comes from the "steady as she goes" school of thought," and "equal opportunity" is the policy we've restored to keep things in divine and pristine order. If you wish to piss off the Lord with your overreaching troublemaking, that is your business, but don't try to include this administration.

As such, White House Inc. has proactively burdened itself with irreversibly dismantling three decades of the legislative hogwash that is deceptively referred to as "affirmative action." This is no easy task, but rest assured that we are committed to preventing all deserving, legacy C students and upstanding, blue-eyed, corporate cubicle warmers from being unjustly displaced by uppity ghetto trash looking for a free ride.

Abortion

While campaigning for the presidency, our CEO committed himself to two important goals: (1) keeping the middle class flush with enough extra pocket change to treat themselves to a celebratory dinner at Sizzler and (2) preserving the sanctity of America's womb boogers. And while "hitting the trifecta" has made the former impossible, He remains deeply committed to the latter.

White House Inc. is patriotically determined to confirm that every time a nasty penis slips into an icky vagina, a little pink fellow or lady will come storming back through that same hirsute hole nine months later. In order to do this, the President has taken aggressive steps to force Americans to bring as many babies into the world as possible, whether they want to or not. Of course, after the infant is slapped and is screaming, we don't much care what they do with it.

Prenatal Tax Reform: President Bush has prepared an Executive Order directing the IRS to allow parents to start writing off their preborn, liquid-breathing tadpole children the same way they do their postborn, air-breathing ones. Once signed, the Order will also require all Americans to begin calculating their age from the moment their father praises the Lord by screaming, "Oh, God! Oh, God!" (conception), rather than the irrelevant event that occurs three-quarters of a fiscal year later when the by-product of this religious ecstasy makes its slimy way into the world.

Outlawing Abortion: The President strongly believes that the ban on the emotionally labeled "partial birth" abortion is an excellent first step in the incremental overturning of the liberal menace Roe v. Wade. The History Channel shows that women, who are by nature little more than nonskim milk–dispensing incubators, have never been able to take care of themselves. That's why the good Lord put menfolk here—to make sure ladies don't go messing around with their insides—which, since they were sprouted off ribs when God was dabbling in cloning, aren't really theirs anyway!

> *Like I always told folks back in Texas before we were about to put down some colored convict, being "pro-life" doesn't have to spoil the fun of getting a kick out of killing folks who aren't inside you.*

In time, with the help of the President's favorite Supreme Court rosary bead counter, Antonin Scalia, the public will come to know an America wherein women are returned to their rightful and Godly positions: barefoot, pregnant, and occasionally missionary. Until then, we must work hard to propose alternatives to vacuuming Junior into a deep red mist. Alternatives such as Christian Indoctrination Work Camps for ghetto mutts, tax money for Nerf, "safety" coat hangers, fertility drug–spiked menthol cigarettes, and prime-time broadcasts of the positive, life-affirming sitcom *Sparky, the Happy Goopy Uterus Globule That Could.*

Health Care

As a White House Inc. employee, you can take pride in the fact that even though America is the world's wealthiest nation, it hasn't succumbed to the socialistic fad of providing its poorest citizens with medical care. You know that our system of medicine is a model of privatization unfettered—with a dazzling ability to parlay life-threatening illness and suffering into second vacation homes for physicians and obsequious pharmaceutical salesmen.

True, a miniscule minority of tens of millions of people who tend to vote for Democrats anyway can't afford health care. Fortunately, as an ardent believer in the powers of the placebo effect, the President is determined to continue making the critically ill feel better by talking about a vague "Patients' Bill of Rights"—which will someday, somehow, grant these statistically inconsequential people the same right as everyone else to be turned away by an HMO that has a cheerful, three-color brochure and a wistful Chapter 11 reorganization plan.

And while a healthy majority of Americans have plentiful access to penicillin scraped off the grout around their shower drains, the President is still concerned that the American health care status quo is threatened by a rising tide of class-action lawsuits that feign indignation over gross negligence, incompetence, and/or ethical atrocities. Trial lawyers like Senator John Edwards, the same, greedy, ambulance stalkers who lack enough political savvy to pay financial homage to the GOP, are ruining our nation's medical profession by encumbering physicians with the stupefying morass of accountability.

> *When I hear wonderful accounts of American ingenuity by poor folks like Kansas City's Ida May Haggerty, who performed her own C-section with nothing more than an X-Acto knife, some barbecue tongs, and a jumbo roll of Bounty, it makes me wonder why we need health care at all!*

~~Social~~ Retirement Security

 From the earliest days of his campaign to recapture the Executive Branch from terrorist-coddling Democrats, George W. Bush has been straightforward in voicing his intention to reinvent the way affluent Americans plan for luxury retirement. Indeed, when He promised to both "modernize" and "reform" Social Security, He wasn't just talking about finally getting those little blue-green cards laminated so they don't turn to mush in your wallet whenever some touchy little lady dumps a highball of Glenmorangie on your lap while pretending to be disgusted by the flattering way you paw her. No, he was talking about the outright dismantling of the ill-conceived system that for an interminable four generations has stood as a shamelessly Socialist obstacle to millions of grannies' freedom to enjoy their deserved twilight diets of Fancy Feast gourmet cat food.

> *Why didn't old LBJ just combine Medicare and Social Security into one program called "Fat Handouts for Lazy Old People Who Can't Take a Hint and Die and Were Too Stupid to Invest Enough Money from Their Six-Figure Jobs or Trust Funds to Retire Comfortably Without Begging Congress for Help Like Some Urine-Stained Hobo."*

Social Security first sprang from the polio-ravaged mind of Franklin Delano Roosevelt—a President so despised and mistrusted by the people, they voted *four times* to imprison him in the White House so they could keep tabs on him. As a wheelchair-bound cripple with no means of supporting himself, Roosevelt was worried about how he would survive once his snaggle-toothed lesbian wife finally got around to divorcing him. Then one night, sleepless with guilt over having invited the Nips to attack Pearl Harbor, he sat upright in bed and cried, "Eureka! I'll create a whole new system of welfare for oldsters that will spawn a fiscal crisis we can blame on Republicans decades after I'm dead!" Today, the value of both Roosevelt the man *and* his ideas are commemorated appropriately—on a lousy thin dime.

Medicare

Medicare is one of the few remaining pieces of pork-barrel legislation passed by the closet Socialist Lyndon Baines Johnson as part of his so-called Great Society initiatives of the mid-1960s. True, Johnson may have been from Texas (and had the longhorn in his trousers to prove it), but at the end of the day, he was just another bleeding-heart liberal who, in spite of his commendable willingness to sacrifice thousands of servicemen's lives so Bob Hope could read cue cards in Southeast Asia, was also treasonously cognizant of the selfish whining of hungry children here at home.

Our CEO understands how popular Medicare is with disadvantaged seniors who are not yet so debilitated by arthritis that they cannot operate a voting machine. That is why He attends at least two photo opportunities per year at turquoise cinder-block Florida nursing homes, gazing into the vacant eyes of the dementia addled, wheezing through an asphyxiating ammonia cloud of Depends fumes, and pretending to listen to crabby complaints and numbing reminiscences over the thunderous roar of the *Golden Girls'* laugh track.

By successfully assuring U.S. geriatrics that He would never exploit their collective snowballing senility for ill-gotten gain, your CEO streamlines the process for realizing the stealth goal of privatizing (eliminating) Medicare completely, thereby fulfilling His obligations to the insurance companies that bankroll your Christmas bonus.

Educasion

> "I do not suggest that you should not have an open mind . . . but don't keep your mind so open that your brains fall out onto the casino floor."
> —William J. Bennett
> Secretary of Education, George H.W. Bush Administration

Today, we find our country's public-education system in a state of crisis. From sea to petroleum-filmed sea, legions of hook-nosed leftists are realizing their goal to roll out radical syllabi stocked with such NPR fairy tales as "evolution" (see p. 121), "heliocentrism," and "Spanish." And all the while, our impressionable children sit powerless, enduring wave after wave of treasonous verbal diarrhea crashing down on their defenseless, little blond buzz cuts.

"No Child Left with an Unwhipped Behind"

President Bush is determined to put an end to this nonsense. On January 8, 2002, He signed the No Child Left Behind Act, which establishes long-overdue accountability in assuring that the math, science, and GameBoy scores of real American boys are just as high as those of their sneaky Oriental classmates. By taking education out of the hands of atheists who believe your great-great-grandpa was a feces-flinging baboon and putting it into the snake-handling hands of fundamentalist parochial schools, we avert a disturbing future in which children of different tax brackets congeal into a repulsive pudding cooked up by ponytailed "educators" who pretentiously caress each vowel even more lovingly than their high priestess Maya Angelou.

More important—and let's be honest for a moment—the quickly imploding public schools are populated overwhelmingly by children whose America-hating parents vote for tree-hugging, pansy-marrying, light-in-the-loafers DemocRATS. As Christians, we know that the sins of the fathers shall be visited upon the sons. And what better way can there be to get back at liberal parents who vote for our competition than making sure their children grow up to shine our children's wingtips with a smile?

Bushie and I were so committed to not leaving a single child behind, that when we moved to D.C., we left both of them behind!

How You Can Help

Just because White House Inc. won't give money to schools that don't have polo teams doesn't mean you can't try. Within five (5) business days of commencing employment at White House Inc., you must return Form 3498-L, designating if you will generously donate more than the standard 5 percent before-tax contribution automatically deducted from your paycheck for the First Lady's Reading Stuff Is Real Important program. As you know, Mrs. Bush has become our nation's most notorious proponent of the radical, all-new school of thought that suggests that teaching and books are—somehow—of help to our nation's young people. To show that her unqualified commitment to the idea of teaching children is just as zealous as was her devotion to actually teaching them,

(Copyright © AFP Corbis.)

Mrs. Bush will donate, along with a portion of your salary, one full percentage point for every full year she tirelessly labored as a teacher[5] from the sale of all of Nancy Reagan's gaudy, lipstick-smeared place settings on eBay.

Revisionist History Alert: With no regard to how our children may view their glorious motherland, public-school teachers stain our nation's spotless history by ignoring the generous corn casseroles the Pilgrims gave recipe-deprived Injuns at the first Thanksgiving to harp on a few brief centuries of land reallocation and smallpox—when everyone knows Injuns would rather have a case of firewater than a million acres of real estate. After all, in all the thousands of years the so-called Native Americans had California and Idaho, did they ever get off their naked, red keisters to strip-mine even one hillside? In spite of this shocking indolence, many teachers are doing their best to turn Injuns into idyllic heroes. Your CEO opposes this unequivocally!

Abstinence-Only Educasion

Our Republicans forefathers, the Puritans, were quite rightly embarrassed by talk about the Lord's most unsavory invention—biology. They knew that contrary to radical European teaching techniques that suggest knowledge is a good thing, the opposite is in fact true. Hence, while colonial teachers spoke in graphic, historically accurate detail about how Cain brutally bludgeoned his brother Abel to death, they carefully sidestepped the awkward acknowledgment of each boy's conception, much less the necessarily incestuous liaisons required to produce ribless Adam's grandchildren. Quite simply, it is polite to talk about procreation by the deboning of a man, but not by the boning of a woman.

☆ **No Trojans lovingly slid onto bananas by salacious health teachers!**

I'm a teacher. Did you know that? Yes, indeedy. I'm a teacher. I teach. Well, not anymore. But I did. I taught. Because that's what teaching is all about!

[5] One (1) year.

> *When I was a young lady, I never had to learn what a darn willy wacker looked like to know I wasn't supposed to go around sitting on them!*

This successful approach to avoiding unpleasant information has set the groundwork for GOP championing of the current "Abstinence Only" craze in our nation's schools. An Abstinence Only curriculum promotes education based purely on aphorisms and Godly misinformation in lieu of so-called facts. Because when it comes to sex, the Devil is in the details. And children don't need to know exactly what it is they are being asked not to do—especially when it involves inserting those "thingies" into somebody's "you-know-what."

☆Success Spotlight: Sue-Jane Helms, Rightsville High School

> *Me and my boyfriend, Hunter, took President Bush's "True Love Waits" pledge this year because we know that God wants me to save my pussy for marriage. Well, Hunter has been so hella supportive and everything, I started thinking he might be, you know, like, queer or something. But then I realized that the power of the Lord is so strong in Hunter, he knows that I respect myself too much to give up my honeypot until he, like, buys me stuff like a house and a ring. Until then, we are totally anal.*

"No Child Left Unsaved": Restoring Prayer to Our Public Schools

Today, an increasingly alarming proportion of children in America's public schools come from inferior religious backgrounds like Hinduism, in which their parents have so many different gods (with so many different arms), it's no wonder their kids are confused. Our CEO believes in helping these young people to simplify their lives by picking the one and only true God, which conveniently comes in three different flavors: Jesus (the friendly God); His Daddy (the angry, powerful God); and the Holy Spirit (the superhero with magical powers God).

☆ **If children are allowed to pee in school, they should be allowed to pray.**

Of course, a barrier to this mission has been liberals opening the floodgates of anti-Christian scorn by using the deceitful weapons of diversity and political correctness to nefariously suggest that our personal beliefs are not vastly superior to everyone else's. As a result, we are all now expected to be so sensitive to the feelings of heretical liars, it has gotten to the point when a teacher can no longer tell a kindergartner he'll be tortured in Hell without getting an angry, unintelligible call from some foreign or colored parent!

As long as there are hungover, legacy-admission students taking Yale midterms, there will always be prayer in school.

President Bush is convinced that the lack of prayer in our public schools was a major factor in rendering our country vulnerable to terrorist attack. It is for this reason that in January 2004, He gathered with prominent GOP Congressmen in the lobby of the Moral Majority headquarters to sign the No Child Left Unsaved Act. This inspired and compassionate legislation codifies our CEO's insistence that going forward, if we continue to allow children to break from their studies to heed the call of Nature and pee, we must also compel them to heed the call of God and get up in front of their little classmates and beg Jesus for lots of cool stuff.

☞ **Policy Pointer:** Feigning Respect for False Religions: Remember, whether Hell-bound youngsters are Muslims, praying to a false, crazy God, or Jews, who are praying to only one-third of a God, who no longer listens to them, it is important to pretend to tolerate their right to make fools of themselves. It is only through flattery that we can cozy up close enough to effectively undermine and replace their so-called sacred beliefs.

A Note on So-Called Evolution

While it goes without saying, it can never be reiterated enough that the most dangerous propaganda ever spawned by cloven-hooved liberal DEMONcrats is the so-called theory of evolution. All scientific theories, of course, come about when Satan cunningly talks matter into acting in a way that contravenes Bible teachings—simply to throw off humans who are less resolute in their faith. The Devil did this when he convinced apples (which had previously cooperated on the testing of humans in Eden) to hurl themselves at Sir Isaac Newton's empty noggin. Later, the Prince of Darkness recruited wicked turtles to convince the radical left-wing animal stalker Charles Darwin into scribbling an opium-fueled epiphany about his great-granddaddy being an orangutan. This nonsense would come to be known as evolution.

Republicans know that scientists have never cared, nor will they ever care, one iota about the "truth," because truth can't be found with a Bunsen burner—only a burning bush.

Indeed, the book of Genesis is quite clear about where human beings came from. Your employer acknowledges that it only took God a few days to create each species separately, and that man didn't evolve from anything other than a few pieces of magic dust the Lord rubbed between his fingers. Yet today, Mr. Darwin's preposterous ramblings are being taught to millions of American public-school children as "fact." President Bush opposes this and is actively doing his righteous best to pull the financial plug on public education before any more impressionable youngsters dismiss the credible account of a talking snake in favor of an outlandish hypothesis of a humping chimp.

If man is just a monkey, is Michael Jackson a slave master for buying Bubbles?

☞ **Policy Pointer:** Pursuant to Executive Order #13309-G, effective January 1, 2006, all public-school instruction in the fuzzy logic so-called disciplines of biology, chemistry, mathematics, and physics will be distilled into a comprehensive three-hour eighth-grade seminar entitled "Secular Mythology."

The War on [Illegal] Drugs

Our CEO understands that the best wars are those waged stealthily against a mysterious and difficult-to-eradicate enemy. Hopefully, the battles drag on indefinitely with few signs of tangible success—and, indeed, despite voluminous evidence indicating they're having the *opposite* of their intended effect. That's why the quarter century–old War on Drugs, while less politically useful these days than its terror-focused sibling, remains a high priority on the President's domestic agenda.

President Bush believes that addiction to luscious, irresistible, illegal drugs is a major cause of hopelessness in America. He knows, albeit definitely not from personal pre-1974 experience, that drugs can almost, but not actually, damage an inherited political career and reduce opulent wealth to a single impotency-inducing desire. As a White House Inc. staffer, you are now part of this righteous crusade and will be working hard with Anheuser-Busch and RJ Reynolds executives to fight non–country club drugs by cutting off supplies and reducing demand through stepped-up executions and the aggressive construction of Black Teen Gulags.

So long as there are nonincarcerated, pubescent, colored boys earning Ramen money off of dimebags, al-Qaeda sleeper cells can and will be constructing nukular bombs in the basement of a FUBU outlet near you.

The Origin of Nancy Reagan's
"Just Say No"

Fellow Republican and reputed fellatio expert Nancy Reagan first employed the wildly inventive phrase "Just Say No" during a 1981 East Room concert. During this now-famous live PBS telecast, Frank Sinatra played a wily practical joke by sprinkling the contents of 300 Sweet'N Low packets on the black lacquer top of Marvin Hamlisch's Steinway. An increasingly distracted Liza Minnelli belted her way through much of "I'm Still Here" before succumbing to temptation and flinging herself, headfirst, onto the piano. Mrs. Reagan, annoyed that her favorite anthem to ornery old broads who can't take a hint was interrupted before its sassy climax, brushed off her cerise taffeta Bill Blass and chided Miss Minnelli by first uttering the now-famous: "Liza May, just say no to drugs!" Nancy's caveat, "Except for pep and diet pills," was rendered inaudible by the coughing brought on by the cloud of sweet, white powder that fell around the room like nuclear winter.

Drugs /drəgz/: n. any one of a number of nonalcoholic, tobacco-free, or discreetly prescribed substances, which when taken internally, produce physiological effects inconsistent with traditional means of ruling class auto-narcosedation.

> *To keep America safe, I'm also working closely with the forty-year-old virgins at NASA to develop supersophisticated gizmos for taking alien fingerprints, antennaeprints, suckerprints, and greasy stump smears. Moving forward, I intend to enforce illegal-alien policy by drafting Tommy Lee Jones and his partner—the colored fella from that* Urkel of Bel Air *show.*

Immigration

While the United States may be a nation of immigrants who arrived poor, tired, and hungry on these shores to find them completely uninhabited by the ancestors of casino operators, our CEO believes that in a post-9/11 world, it is imperative that we revisit the suspiciously open-armed ideals of that libertine French hussy, the Statue of Liberty. Therefore, short of outright sealing our borders—infinitely ideal though that may be—the President feels that the following minor tweaking of existing INS and border-patrol policy will serve to temporarily protect our tender heartland:

Keeping Out Islamoids: Islam has paid good money to be designated "The Official Religion of International Terrorists" (see p. 151). Islamoids pray by strapping dynamite to themselves and assuming a gaseous and liquid form. While Muslamic attitudes about how to deal with pushy women are much more attractive than our own, it is nevertheless in America's best interest to keep as many of them out of the country as possible. For those likely terrorists already within our borders, the President has directed the INS to share its Arabiac-tracking database with the Homeland Security SWAT division. That way, when a Hindu-looking bigmouth cracks a 9/11 joke at a Denny's in Florida, we can take the bastard down with a single headshot when he eventually rolls into a Mississippi 7-Eleven to trade anti-American banter with his compatriot working the Diet Dr. Pepper Slurpee machine.

Keeping Out Mexicans: America has lived peacefully alongside Mexicanistas ever since we violently seized 20 percent of their country and started calling it Texas. And while since then we've been willing to look the other way as they bloodied themselves shimmying under razor-wire border fences to steal all our good janitorial sciences careers from the coloreds, this can no longer be. With President Bush having presided over a historic rise in chronic, persistent unemployment, it now behooves America to keep Mexicans out, so that our own, eminently more qualified PhDs, MBAs, and laid-off molecular bioengineers can know the pride-inducing joy of scrubbing floors, trimming hedges, and picking errant pubic hairs off Burger King urinal cakes.

Keeping Out Coloreds: While White House Inc. maintains a stated policy against racial profiling, it is difficult to ignore mounting evidence suggesting that most coloreds are, at least partially, African in nature. As any American male who grew up in the '40s and '50s with their parents' *National Geographic*s can tell you, Africa is chock-full of inky women with skinny boobs and ivory-toothed smiles who store CorningWare in their lips and earlobes. But what was once an innocent land of clandestine masturbatory fodder has turned into a hotbed of both terrorism and AIDS. (Who knew so many Muslim homosexuals lived in one place?) Therefore, going forward, it is the position of this administration to sharply curtail the influx of immigrants from Africa—which for the purposes of maintaining INS procedural simplicity—shall be defined to also include all Caribbean islands, Manhattan north of 104th Street, and Brazil—which we're now told has blacks, too (referred to herein as "Greater Africa").

Keeping Out Orientals: The President is genuinely fond of Orientals. He once visited his parents in their homeland and often marvels openly about the fact that it was these same, dwarfish, funny-talking mathletes who invented carpeting, Hello Kitty, and radiation sickness. He also loves their exotic "Wok 'n Roll" cuisine—especially #5, #17, and #44. Unfortunately, after more than a century of unfettered immigration by Asiatics, far too many blocks of American ghettos have been overrun by reasonably priced fruit stands, horny karaoke singers, and viola-wielding honor students who make it impossible for Caucasian cheerleaders who are full of pep to get into accredited schools. As such, the President has ordered their influx be sharply curtailed, lest so many needle-eyed folks leave their native countries that America's Nike factories not be adequately staffed by nimble-fingered, $1/week nine-year-olds.

Keeping Out Communists: America may be scrotum deep in the War on Terror, but President Bush has no memory of our Cold War enemies formally surrendering. As such, we must remain vigilant. And though Senator Joe McCarthy cannot be here with us today as we wrap ourselves in the flag and denounce our CEO's critics as faggoty Hollywood pinkos, we can still look to his shining example of the dizzying power of xenophobic jingoism. That is why, effective September 12, 2001, White House Inc. immigration policy was formally adjusted to encourage legislative emulation of not only Joe McCarthy and his coltish doppelgänger Ann Coulter, but *any* husky baritone demagogue with balls big and hairy enough to walk up to anybody he doesn't agree with and violently poke the leftist, foreigner-loving, America-hating, slander-spouting, treason-talking vermin in the eye and bellow, "COMMIE GET OUT!"

A Note on Pandering to Wetbacks Who Vote: From time to time, it may be necessary for our CEO to make shallow political overtures to America's libidinous Hispano-Ricans, who have recently overtaken the other coloreds to become the largest servant and valet-parker class. Therefore, DO NOT BE ALARMED should you see President Bush doing any of the following in front of a rolling camera: (a) speaking broken Mexican; (b) cruising the beltway in a salsa-blasting, neon-festooned 1974 Impala; (c) posing with his little brown nephews and niece (court appearance schedules permitting).

Did You Know? When ragtag, disreputable foreigners first started arriving on our far-too-welcoming shores, there were still subways, railroads, and sewers to be built. Nowadays though, we have nearly 3 million Mexicans for every flower bed, but only a handful of Irish scullery maids for each Upper East Side luxury co-op!

"Don't Ask, Don't Tell" Revisited

The budget-surplus nightmare spawned by the previous administration may have squandered America's tax dollars on a giant, useless savings account, but it also had one positive result: enabling our CEO to allocate several billion dollars to researching how best to cleanse our military of the dangerous liberal trend called "homosexuality." In early 2002, the President recruited a representative group of those who are most vexed by homosexual behavior (married Southern Baptist organists and choir directors) and tasked them with finding the best way to exterminate American gayism before every last one of our schoolchildren becomes so corrupted, they wind up wearing a studded leather thong on a parade float somewhere.

> *Our primary concern in saying it's okay to be gay in the military is that there might come a day when everyone decides to become a homosexual, if only for the clothes. If that happens, there'll be no one left to make baby Marines, and in eighteen years or so, we'll be hard-pressed to kill Arabs if our infantry is just a bunch of graying sissies waving around pearl-handled Saturday night specials!*

After nearly two years of pouring over detailed photo dossiers indicating that thousands of enlisted Liberaces are staring at countless different shapes and sizes of naked penises bouncing around in our military showers, the President's team agreed that—short of loading those swishy creatures into boxcars for one-way trips to Canada—America's best hope for eliminating military faggotry lies instead within the framework of the existing "Don't Ask, Don't Tell" policy.

Verily, it doesn't take John Ashcroft's honorary degree from Bob Jones University to be able to tell a queer by his lisp or the bounce in his combat boots. Therefore, going forward, if a sergeant hears an effeminate soldier limply squeak, "YETH THIR!" while holding his rifle like a Bob Fosse bowler, that soldier has just voluntarily applied for active duty on the front lines of combat. We've simply given Don't Ask, Don't Tell a few Compassionately Conservative tweaks. You don't ask us why the rate in homo casualties has dramatically spiked, and we won't tell you why.

The Right to Bear Arms

 As a tireless defender of the Second Amendment to the Constitution, your CEO firmly believes that every American must have unfettered access to weapons of micro and medium destruction—whether he be man or boy, college graduate or special-ed dropout, lucid hatemonger or bloodthirsty Alzheimer's vegetable.

> *Our Founding Fathers clearly predicted a future in which the definition of "arms" would stretch well beyond five-foot-long, black-powder muskets capable of firing one round every three minutes, and most definitely include easily concealable, fully automatic micro-howitzers capable of decimating a filled-to-capacity high school auditorium in seconds flat.*

Because of his clear position on gun ownership, the President enjoys the support of the National Rifle Association—and, as such, sleeps soundly in the knowledge that its millions of dues-paying, utterly nonparanoid members are amassing the personal arsenals of AK-47s, Uzis, and rocket-propelled grenade launchers they need to keep their double-wide mobile homes safe from all manner of thieves, coloreds, and jack-booted federal thugs.

The President opposes any and all gun control legislation that might represent a step toward a future in which a big-balled, blue-eyed frontiersman is not free to patriotically fondle his aftermarket-modified Bushmaster while writhing naked in a puddle of fluoropolymer revolver lubricant, then drink himself into the kind of homici-dal depression that can only be relieved by taking out a few dozen Costco shoppers.

The Homeless

Like Big Foot is to Appalachia, or Chupacabra is to Hispano-Rico, the urban myth of homeless-ness has deep roots in Washington, D.C. As recently as a quarter century ago, bleeding-heart number-crunchers deep within the bowels of federal office buildings tried to hoodwink another visionary Republican President, Ronald Wilson Reagan, into buying the preposterous notion that not only were there Americans who did not own oceanside vacation homes, but that some crippled war veterans were beg-ging for change and sleeping in *refrigerator boxes.* In steadfastly pooh-poohing these allegations, regardless of whatever so-called proof accompanied them, President Reagan exposed this entire socioeconomic topic for what it was—wholly unsuitable for pleasant dinner conversation. Today, President Bush stands in kindred denial with former President Reagan, who had he not been permanently hypnotized by the Cartoon Network, would most certainly have joined your CEO in denouncing this type of destructive, divisive, and utterly dishonest manipulation of the facts. For just as homelessness was a liberal myth of the 1980s, so too is it today, along with any other stuff that liberals say needs the money that is already patriotically earmarked for building Ospreys, JDAMs, and money-market accounts for our Pioneer- and Ranger-level donors.

Let's get those darned shelters shut down already so these homeless folks can start living up to their name!

NOTE: The aforementioned policy statement shall in no way be construed to imply that it is hypocritical for our CEO to exercise presidential prerogative by holding annual photo ops serving frozen fish-stick Thanksgiving dinners to smelly soup-kitchen leeches—who greedily suck at the soft potbelly of wealth that was rightfully bequeathed to We the Chosen by our omnipotent Lord.

Corporate Ethics

This administration is pro–big business. Your CEO believes in smaller, more effective government: less SEC, FDA, and all those other boring-ass bureaucrat wet dreams thought up by nonmillionaire, non–landed gentry creeps who are always getting in the way of His rightful and deserved financial progress.

Unfortunately, in response to fleeting public interest in a few petty, harmless infractions by His intimately close pals at Enron, WorldCom, and Arthur Andersen, the President had no choice but to sign Executive Order #13271 on July 9, 2002. This action, which established a Corporate Fraud Task Force, makes a point of emphasizing that all kinds of common practices that were already illegal are now super-extra-turbo-illegal—and President Bush made them that way!

Consistent with its mandate, the President's Corporate Fraud Task Force wasted no time in meeting with corporate executives over a martini lunch to draw up a new code of American corporate ethics, which had been allowed to deteriorate so shamefully under the regime of Billary Clinton.

UNITED STATES OF AMERICA
REVISED CODE OF CORPORATE ETHICS AND RESPONSIBILITY

Standard of Conduct: The business of American Corporations must be conducted with ~~honesty, integrity and openness~~ *devoted, profit-driven zeal,* and with respect for the ~~human rights and interests~~ *reduced overhead* of each employee. They shall similarly respect ~~the legitimate~~ *any* interests and share valuations of those businesses with whom they have ~~relationships~~ *impending mega-mergers.*

Obeying the Law: American Corporations are required to ~~comply with the laws and regulations of the countries in which they operate~~ *promptly notify the folks at immigration of any suspicious cleaning staff with a weakness for Mont Blanc pen and pencil sets.*

Consumers: American Corporations must be committed to providing branded products and services that consistently ~~offer value~~ *generate revenue* in terms of ~~price and quality~~ *executive compensation beyond the jurisdictional reach of federal bankruptcy courts,* and which ~~are safe for their intended use~~ *may or may not be snake oil and/or highly toxic.* Products and services will be ~~accurately and properly~~ *seductively* labeled, advertised, and communicated, *preferably with an abundance of ripe and willing bosom.*

Employees: American Corporations shall be committed to the semblance of diversity in a working environment. They shall recruit, employ, and promote employees on the sole basis of their ~~qualifications and abilities~~ *golf handicap, Good Old Boy Network connections, appreciation for good-natured humor at the expense of coloreds, women, and homos, and the ability to fill any awkward silence with an unbroken litany of twenty-year-old baseball statistics and NFL scores.* American Corporations must be committed to ~~safe and healthy~~ *productive* working conditions for all employees *regardless of age, height, or number of remaining fingers,* ~~and will not use any form of forced, compulsory or child labor.~~ Furthermore, they shall work closely with employees to ~~develop and enhance each individual's skills and capabilities~~ *root out union organizers* and ~~respect the dignity of the individual and the right of employees to freedom of association~~ *conserve office supplies.*

Conflicts of Interests: All American Corporation executives are expected to ~~avoid~~ *be discreet in all* personal activities and financial dealings that could ~~conflict with their responsibilities to the company~~ *reflect poorly on the Executive Branch, which is already bending every law it possibly can to keep itself and its friends out of prison.* Furthermore, American Corporation executives must ~~not seek gain for themselves or others through misuse of their positions~~

deliver blistering verbal warnings to any company accountant who is caught absentmindedly reporting "debt" as "revenue."

Shareholders: The CEOs of American Corporations must conduct their operations in accordance with ~~internationally accepted principles of good corporate~~ *Skull & Bones Spring Break Keg Fund* governance and will provide ~~timely, regular and reliable information~~ *highly compensated cover story interviews* ~~on their activities, structure, financial situation and performance~~ *extolling their capitalistic acumen* to all ~~shareholders~~ *top-shelf business periodicals, such as* Forbes *and* Money.

Community Involvement: American CEOs must strive to ~~be a trusted corporate citizen~~ *donate exclusively to Republican candidates as a means to ensure that when violent class warfare inevitably erupts, their all-white boards of directors are protected by Delta Force and Patriot Missiles,* and to fulfill their responsibilities to ~~the societies and communities in which we operate~~ *graciously open up their 60,000-sq.-ft. summer home(s) for GOP fund-raising events and/or Enemies of the State detention camps.*

Public Activities: American Corporations are encouraged to promote and defend their ~~legitimate business interests~~ *right to give out seven-figure bonuses to executives who really really deserve them and/or keep their mouths shut,* and to cooperate with ~~governments~~ *the GOP* and other organizations, both directly and through bodies such as ~~trade associations~~ *the Christian Coalition and Mr. Cheney's "Rape California" energy consortium* in the ~~development~~ *blockage* of proposed *Democratic* legislation and/or regulations that may ~~affect legitimate business interests~~ *inhibit stock portfolio appreciation and/or wholesale exploitation of workers who vote Democrat.* ~~American Corporations neither support political parties nor contribute to the funds of groups whose activities are calculated to promote party interests.~~

Business Integrity: American Corporations do not *publicly* give or receive, whether directly or indirectly, ~~kickbacks, bribes or other~~ improper advantages for business or financial gain *that could possibly come to the attention of the non-FOX News media without first establishing a sterling reputation for plausible deniability.* All accounting records and supporting documents must ~~accurately~~ describe and reflect the ostensible nature of any ~~underlying~~ *conspicuous* transactions. Furthermore, no ~~undisclosed or unrecorded~~ offshore account, fund, or asset will be ~~established or maintained~~ *used to hedge political bets by supporting baby-killing, fudgepacker-kissing Democrats.*

Hate-Crimes Legislation

On June 11, 2002, Senate Republicans, acting on direct orders from our CEO, killed debate on the Local Law Enforcement Enhancement Act (LLEEA), effectively putting the brakes on further proliferation of so-called hate-crimes legislation. President Bush believes that having the government pass laws to tell people that they can't hate homos or hebes or coons or chinkatronics is just plain ridiculous. We Americans have long cherished the right to hate anyone different—even when we can't quite put our finger on why they are so damned annoying.

Over the years, our media has joined hands with our military and its suppliers to help us hate just about every kind of foreigner at one time or another: the Spanish, Germans (twice, but, truly, was that enough?), Japs (we still have the concentration camp to prove it), French (eternally), Russians (until we introduced them to capitalism through bankruptcy), Chinese (until they stumbled upon using slave labor to produce all those fabulous plastic trinkets we can't get enough of), Koreans (the mean, Fido-poaching ones), Vietnamese (the sneaky, war-winning ones), Iranians (after our puppet) and Iraqis (during our puppet),. Of course, this list does not include the fabulous people of Saudi Arabia, who under no circumstances (no matter how many American skyscrapers they raze or women they behead) are ever to be disparaged because of all the cool oil contracts they have with the Bush family.

Today however, in the poisonous wake of Brown v. Board of Education, we live in a country where people are forced to be somewhat more discreet about their hatred of those who flaunt their differentness. Even so, the maddeningly interfering liberals are not satisfied. They are still running around the country trying to get new laws passed that make it a crime to hate all kinds of disgusting, annoying people, thereby undermining every God-fearing, fundamentalist Christian Klansman's freedom to hate whomever they want. Besides, hate is an emotion our CEO respects. Without it, He never could have experienced the kind of violent determination that makes it possible for a tongue-tied alcoholic to take down Ann Richards and Bill Clinton's handpicked successor as revenge for the way they both politically humiliated His daddy.

The Space Program

Scientists (most of whom are atheists) often speak of outer space as "the final frontier." Well, it's not. Space is where God lives, and the President believes that we need to respect His privacy. In fact, our solar system is God's front porch, where He likes to sit cradling a double-barreled Winchester and reading Louis L'Amour novels in Hebrew. When we stray too far from the surface of the Earth, God becomes angry, and squeezes off a tempest of meteor buckshot. The President is confident that every space-related disaster—from *Apollo 1* to the shuttle *Columbia*—is directly attributable to having interrupted God in the middle of a good chapter.

Of course, the President has seen the fancy, Hollywood-style photos of deep space taken by that giant telescope upon which some misguided liberal predecessor squandered billions that could have been better wasted here on Earth. He thinks the photos are neat. They remind him of the Spencer Gifts black-light posters that bedecked his daughters' dormitory rooms. But outside of applications in military rockets and plastic spatula–friendly cookware, the President isn't particularly interested in such worthless space "science" as monitoring the stupefyingly incremental melting of the ice caps—but he is willing to concede that "it's sort of nifty how ass biscuits float out of your butt in zero gravity."

Therefore, the President prefers to focus our energies not on pointless, deep-space exploration and interplanetary travel, but on practical, closer-to-home space stuff like federally subsidized Clear Channel satellites, orbiting Darth Vader Armageddon cannons, and geosynchronous spy cameras capable of super-zooming onto pro-baseball games and transmitting them directly to Air Force One. He is also deeply committed to the defense industry–conceived Wholesale Militarization of Space Initiative, which will fill our stratosphere with the thousands of airborne nuclear missile silos we'll need to protect Earth from otherwise inevitable annihilation by asteroids, alien invaders, and all the foreign governments that don't have trillions of dollars to blow on such super-amazing death gadgets.

The Environment

 Since receiving a sweeping mandate from the 47.8 percent of the 51.3 percent of the population that cared enough to vote, your CEO has been proactive in conceiving forward-thinking and creatively entitled environmental legislation. "Clear Skies" demands that GOP-tithing factories reduce their toxic emissions just as soon as somebody, somewhere, invents fabulous, inexpensive "new technologies" to do it. "Healthy Forests" aggressively prevents grass and brush fires by felling thousand-year-old trees and shipping them off to Home Depot as redwood picnic tables. Moving forward, look for more inspired environmental activism, including the "Pristine Waters" Fecal Coliform Protection Initiative and the "Bountiful Creatures" Wholesale Wildlife Extermination Act of 2007.

White House Inc. Environmental Policy Hallmarks

1. The Bush Administration is committed to reducing the increase in sooty phlegm emissions from asthmatic children by .002 percent by the year 2075.

2. The Bush Administration promises efficient and speedy recycling of crude oil–soaked sea gull and otter pelts into high-octane, SUV-friendly vroom-vroom juice.

3. The Bush Administration is determined to keep America's groundwater safe from exposure to coal, which must be aggressively extracted from the earth and disposed of in clean, modern enviro-furnaces.

4. The Bush Administration will use every means at its disposal to protect Americans from the less-than-genetically-perfect produce of organic farmers, the annoying twirling of New Age power windmills, and the insidious dangers of solar-energy poisoning.

If you give a Third World peasant a plastic can of gasoline, he barely has enough to self-immolate. But if you teach him to clear-cut his rain forest and lay a thousand miles of forty-eight-inch pipe, he can keep America in riding-mower fuel for an entire hour of his otherwise inconsequential lifetime!

5. The Bush Administration will work diligently to protect the natural habitats of noble species such as the spotted moth, all American Kennel Club breeds (except femmy teacup poodles), and the Three Mile Island scorpion trout.

> *Liberals are all gung-ho about Charlie Darwin's theories when it comes to making folks a monkey's uncle, but when it comes to endangered species, they don't want so-called natural selection to take its course. There is a mighty good reason why a forest or an owl is endangered. They are pathetically weak. And who are we to interfere with Nature? It's like when I'm driving through the Maryland suburbs. I'm not necessarily saying I ever have, but if I were to run over a child when I'm in a rush to get to a 10:30 wash 'n set hair appointment, aren't I just giving "natural selection" a gentle boost by killing off something too stupid to notice a car running a red light? When I ask secular humanists that question, they always gawk at me with a weird look because they don't have a good answer. I tell you, there is no sport in stumping liberals!*

6. The Bush Administration will move aggressively to combat the supposed influence of cow farts on the totally made-up "greenhouse effect"—offering generous incentives to the Ponderosa Steakhouse to advance its important work in the bovine management sector.

7. The Bush Administration will act quickly and without regard to cost in stamping out "global warming"—and all other objectionable references in scientific reports by the EPA.

8. The Bush Administration will propose billions in research funding for eco-friendly, utterly viable hydrogen-powered cars and super-spaceman, personal jet packs, which before being summarily slashed in the opening minutes of congressional budget negotiations, will briefly set the hearts of fat, clammy, *Star Trek* nerds aflutter.

9. The Bush Administration will tirelessly champion environmental freedoms, like the freedom to dig a hole in your yard and have it fill up with flammable, phosphorescent ooze.

10. The Bush Administration will urge Congress to pass the Green Earth Day Act, in which we will take the tired, liberal concept of a Victimized Mother Earth and recast the planet as an Empowered Hooker Earth, begging to be drilled!

Public Service

You will, from time to time, hear all of us who toil at White House Inc. referred to officially as "public servants." It is of course perfectly natural to laugh mockingly and/or recoil in revulsion at the preposterous implications of that label, which is used merely to mollify voters with the comforting illusion of accountability. As Republicans, we are no more servants of the public than we are helpless slaves to mercy or its weak-willed cousin, decency.

In a limber turn of semantic acrobatics, President Bush prefers, instead, to dexterously shift the emphasis of that "service" thing (with all the humiliating fellatio connotations that spring immediately to mind) to the public. That is why, in His 2002 State of the Union Address, He announced the creation of the USA Freedom Corps—which takes all the dumb, Democrat-created, anti-freedom corps like AmeriCorps, Senior Corps, and the Peace Corps, and puts them under an enormous, all-new umbrella of compassionately conservative bureaucracy. Indeed, by appropriating the entire spectrum of existing volunteerism, giving it a freedomtastic new name, and dressing it up in miles and miles of star-spangled bunting, the President has been daringly proactive in simulating the appearance of crafting meaningful public-service policy, while really drop-kicking several more expensive programs into the festering landfill of liberal humanitarianism.

All the above notwithstanding, in the final weeks preceding any election, employees are strongly encouraged to join the President whenever He is photographed hammering a few shingles onto the roof of another new palatial voucher school. PLEASE NOTE: Under no circumstances should these wholly original acts of presidential decency invoke comparisons to a certain has-been, bucktoothed peanut farmer who ought to be cashing in on the lecture circuit instead of playing Bob Vila for a bunch of ex–crack whores and other trash wisely abandoned by a nose-holding Lord.

☆ **TIP: Since mixed company is an unfortunately unavoidable reality in Washington, D.C., it's wise to affect an attitude of prostrate humility when publicly discussing your "work" for "the people." That's just good politics— and a source of mirth to your fellow workers.**

Bipartisanship

 Throughout his presidential campaign, George W. Bush proudly trumpeted His gubernatorial reputation for cooperation with Lone Star State Democrats and solemnly pledged to infuse the political culture of Washington, D.C., with the same brand of hickory-smoked, baby back rib–style bipartisanship. While this did not alarm D.C. Republicans, who knew that a Texas Democrat is about as leftist as your average Utah prison warden, the voters were nevertheless enamored by this professed commitment to playing nice.

Unfortunately, upon arriving in the U.S. capital, the President was dismayed to discover that Congress is awash in a spineless, fruit-loop variety of Democrats—too few of whom know the character-building struggle of pulling oneself up by the loafer tassels to claim the fortune that's his trustafarian birthright. Populated primarily by obstructionists and filibusterers, the Capitol Hill Democratic Caucus is hopelessly gridlock-happy, content to sit around complaining, knitting hemp-twine hacky sacks, and trying to steal faith-based tax dollars to subsidize preteen abortion hobby kits.

Sadly, despite countless sincere gestures of openness to congressional Democrats, the President, disappointingly, has never met with a response that rose to a polite level of respectful worship. As such, going forward, "bipartisanship" shall be defined to mean "the occasional posing for news-media cameras with tax-drunk America-haters too obstinate and/or stupid to jump at the chance to drop trou, grab ankles, and squeeze when it hurts."

> *Back in Austin, I pretended to get along real good with Democrats. Of course, once I got to Washington, I told Tom DeLay to fumigate the Texas legislature and send those little cockroach pussies scurrying into Oklahoma and New Mexico!*

Working with Fiscal-Restraint Republicans

As a Republican, President Bush is blessed by a public that pays attention to His labeling Democrats as "big spenders" without mordantly dwelling on His own propensity to splurge like Michael Jackson at a Thai black-market orphanage. Indeed, His inspired, new fiscal program demands America never be too chicken to rack up a teensy-weensy bit of multigazillion-dollar debt in exchange for keeping its babies safe from getting fed into wood chippers by armies of anthrax-covered, Arabiac demon people.

> *I keep telling those anal accounting nitwits that we're not running the goddamned federal budget on Quicken®—it doesn't have to add up, folks!*

The President believes it's time to confront silly governmental hang-ups about "debt" head-on. Budgets are for the bottom 99 percent—inconsequential nobodies with nothing better to do than balance every last penny in their sorry little checkbooks. Well, there's an old adage that says, "You've got to spend money to make money." President Bush's version goes, "You've got to spend money to keep spending money to not care whether or not you ever make money so long as unemployed Harry and Helen Hotpocket are so busy crapping their drawers over the latest terrorism color that they keep voting for you even though they've defaulted on their mortgage and are shopping for underwear at the Salvation Army."

Republicans who aren't on board with this inspired Reagan-like fiscal program are demonstrating an unfortunate geek-with-an-HP-calculator inclination toward the so-called exact sciences of accounting and mathematics. Any such fiscal-worrywart politician can forget about having President Bush support his pet spending bills, let alone appear at campaign rallies to tell his clueless constituents that he's a "good man" who "loves freedom" and does a "fabulous job."

VI.
FOREIGN
POLICY

INTRODUCTION

For much of the latter half of the twentieth century, American foreign policy was shaped largely by the so-called Cold War, a conflict that was won so triumphantly by your CEO's father in a heroic, diplomatic marathon of watching Mikhail Gorbachev on CNN. Then, inexplicably, throughout most of the '90s, U.S. international relations were built instead upon Clintonian wet dreams of a global utopia where braless hippies in tie-dyed sarongs spiral danced the day away, and America's military might was squandered saving oil-poor nations from themselves.

Today, your CEO has thankfully brought America back to reality, fashioning an all-new foreign-policy agenda based solely on an eternal crusade against a spectral and unspecific EVIL. By defeating EVIL, EVIL-doers, those who harbor EVILdoers, those who could maybe become EVIL, or merely even those who look EVIL, think EVIL thoughts, or have an EVIL axis to grind—President Bush is gloriously deploying U.S. soldiers and cannons on a real-world Risk board so that one day soon, every last continent will know the joy of American-style democracy—even if that means killing every last Godless bastard who doesn't want it.

"Nation building" was the centerpiece of my foreign policy platform during the 2000 campaign. That's one of dozens of reasons I won in an unprecedented landslide!

International Consensus Building

When aggressively pursuing any international policy that purports to help any country other than His own, President Bush believes it is sometimes useful to create the pleasant illusion of global backing. For instance, before making a unilateral preemptive strike against a desert armpit nation that was fiscally and militarily crippled by a decade of United Nations sanctions, your CEO assembled a "coalition" of over thirty-five countries—including some you may have even heard of, like the invaluable Nicaragua.

In return for suppressing the will of their peoples, wired cash, and offering up official, if not popular, hosannas of nonmilitary support, several of these countries' leaders were handsomely rewarded with wired cash and an all-expense-paid trip to Crawford, Texas—complete with one night's sweet dreams on the full-size pullout of the President's rec-room Naugahyde sectional.

After haggling with Turkey for two weeks over whether America would buy each of their citizens a BMW with leather interiors or just leather-trimmed interiors, I realized that we already had the best Iraq-invading coalition money would buy. So I told them to stick their tongues up a dead camel's ass.

Treaties

Your CEO has invested considerable intellectual energy in the development of a complex and nuanced system that categorizes everything in the world as either "Good for America" or "Bad for America." As a rule, treaties are Bad for America. And by America, President Bush of course means His patriotic partners over at Halliburton, Raytheon, ExxonMobil, Bechtel, and Philip Morris—recently renamed Altria, which is Latin for "Class-Action Lawsuit Evasion."

Even if it's just us and Lichtenstein, it's still a coalition!

It's important that people understand that so-called treaties—whether they be the Kyoto Climate Control Accord, the World Health Tobacco Control Treaty, or some silly antiballistic missile agreement—aren't really about attempting to effect fundamental changes that will have far-reaching benefits for our entire species. No, what they're really about is the rest of the world's bitter, inferior nations getting all up in America's face and trying to demand it join them in the

International Losers Club. It's like America is the captain of the football team, and all those other countries are the pencil-dicked A/V club dorks pressuring it to sign some dumb church pledge not to score a juicy slice of poontang on prom night. Our CEO says "nuts" to that.

☆ Old Europe Policy

> **This administration does not recognize treaties signed by any so-called American President who had to rely on the popular vote to get power. After all, if he is that lame at home at getting his way with Americans, how can we expect him to cheat foreigners out of stuff?**

Your CEO's foreign policy is informed by the knowledge that "Old Europe" countries such as France and Germany are rich, weak, and arrogant. For the most part, they're a hodge-podge of sauerkraut-slurping, Colonel Klink–sounding anal retentives and fey Marcel Marceau cowards who are bitter as hell that all their best and brightest shipped out to America way back when, then started making even better liquid-fuel rockets and wine once they got here. Old Europe spent the past sixty years building a cushy socialist welfare state with money they didn't have to spend on a military—because America had defense covered for them. And today, though Old Europeans are too lazy to even make babies, they still manage to stir up the energy to impudently moan and complain every time their benevolent protector gets itchy to take its Cadillac of a military out for a wholly necessary joyride.

France-Bashing Standards and Guidelines

The French have always been a thorn in the side to everyone—except Hitler. In recent years, however, their pompous misapprehension that they actually matter has taken a decidedly annoying turn. Therefore President Bush has directed all staffers to adopt the following France-bashing standards and guidelines:

1. All White House Inc. staffers will immediately discontinue use of the word "French." For example, henceforth, that overly sweet, bloody liquid slathered on yellowed iceberg lettuce at Shoney's shall be "Prancing Snail Swallower Dressing"; those greasy sticks of carbohydrates and sodium kept warm for hours under heat lamps at McDonald's shall be "Beret-Wearing Pansy Fries" (and shall no longer be available in any size other than "embarrassingly small"); and restaurants throughout the land will begin serving "Unbathed Asshole Onion Soup."

2. Staffers shall promptly initiate a boycott of the "French kiss"—replacing it with *patriotic* expressions of affection such as the "Texas Uvula Wallop" and the "Dixieland Stinky Finger."

3. Upon sipping from any glass or bottle of inferior French wine in a restaurant, all employees are hereby directed to spit it onto the floor before shrieking that the imported beverage was either "too flinty" or "indistinguishable from a rancid slick of year-old poodle menses" before loudly ordering a refreshing 48-oz. Gallo Peach Liebfraumilch slushy as a replacement.

4. All summer interns, upon returning to college, must dispense with the folly of studying the pathetic "soft philosophies" of Voltaire, Sartre, and Descartes—and begin aggressively indoctrinating themselves to the profound, righteous, and less tediously cerebral works of Hannity, Rumsfeld, Noonan, and The Rock.

5. Moving forward, staffers should encourage journalists and historians alike to incinerate any liberal textbooks that incorrectly assert that the French saved the colonists' ragtag, shoeless asses at Yorktown during America's noble fight for independence from those charmingly irascible and currently endearing limeys (a struggle now rendered ironically moot by Britain's decision to fork over what little sovereignty they didn't give to the European Socialist Union to the U.S. State department).

☆ New Europe Policy

New Europe, which includes such economic and cultural powerhouses as Poland, the Czech (pronounced "Check") Republic, and Bulgaria, represents the future of American international relations. Its residents, while still generally funny-talking, have proven themselves worthy of America's foreign-policy largesse by demonstrating a commendable eagerness to shed their prideful garments, assume the position to be fitted with one of President Bush's shiny patent-leather saddles, and cooperatively muzzle any girly squeals when the spurs dig in!

☆ Middle East Policy

Despite your CEO's early best efforts to ignore it out of existence, the ongoing conflict between the Israeloids and Palestinos has nevertheless become the focus of America's Middle Eastern agenda. Indeed, without President Bush's selfless intervention, the eternal blood feud—spawned by Bill Clinton's perverted quest for "A Piece in the Middle East"—might destabilize the entire region, thereby raising the possibility that America's thirst for cheap, plentiful Arabiac oil might not be quenched. Worse yet, Americans might be forced to pay market-driven prices for the stuff and have to start driving around in two-cylinder, Korean rice burners.

Instead of blabbing about everything we're doing wrong-o in Iraqistan, why can't those liberal media fruits report about all the millions of perfectly nice cars and ambulances that totally DON'T explode?

The President is tired of hearing about those uppity, toga-wearing Yasser Arafat people blowing themselves into bacon bits while Christ-killing Zionoids build chintzy, poorly landscaped new houses on disputed patches of worthless desert. As such, he is making a one-time exception to His usual strict policy of not interfering with biblical prophecies of chaos, death, and destruction. The result, a veritable tour de force of diplomatic cartography called the Road Map to Middle East Peace, is certain to extricate these people from their eternal quagmire of politically annoying hatred and violence. And if not, Rummy's Crusaders will not hesitate to put the whole damned region in a righteous Christian headlock.

Your CEO's Road Map to Middle East Peace

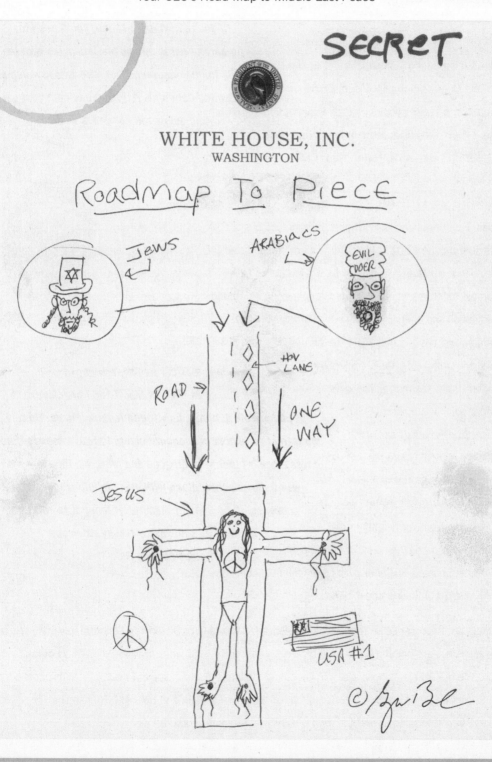

☆ Oriental Policy

Although supposedly a rich tapestry of ancient cultures, the Orient is basically Japan, China, and all the rest of the yellow people, most of whom don't even merit their own restaurants in the phone book. In keeping with this self-evident truth, your CEO has formulated his Asian policy accordingly:

> *If you're anything like me, you'll need to be careful not to mix up the Japansies with the Gandhi Injuns. Just remember, one eats raw fish and puts a red dot on his flag, and one eats goat guts and puts a red dot on his woman!*

Japan: President Bush believes that Japan's future is fated to be largely symbolic. The sun may be rising in their land, but in Washington, D.C., it's set. As a nation once conquered and occupied by the United States military, Japan serves as a shining example for others who have tasted America's boot. Indeed, by adopting a U.S.-authored constitution and offering up their poor women as GI love trampolines, the Japanese laid the ground-work for cultivating their trademark modern traits: technological savvy, xenophobia, and a susceptibility to cartoon-induced seizures. Should America's more recent conquests like Afghanistan and Iraq emulate Japan closely, they too will reach similar heights—per-haps even knowing the honor of having a President named Bush bestow a ceremonial lapful of vomit on their prime minister.

> *My poppy was our country's envoy to Red China back in '74 and '75. He and his close, but completely platonic, lady friend Jennifer Fitzgerald told me many fabulous stories about Peking. I always used to think it was a scary place with dragons and MSG, but they told me it was a real discreet place with many fabulous romantic getaways. Of course, my mom never thought so, which is maybe why she was so cranky when she came back to D.C.*

China: U.S. Representative Tom DeLay—America's Orkin Man of Diplomacy—once sagely observed that China's rulers are nothing but a pack of "decrepit tyrants." And while privately your CEO couldn't agree more, He nevertheless chose wisely in becoming the latest in a long line of Republicrat Presidents adhering to the One China doctrine, which mandates: "Engage, Contain, and Buy, Buy, Buy All That Cheap Stuff (Like Water Pistols and Livers) Churned Out By Their Convict Laborers."

Yes, China may be a volatile and unpredictable force in the world. And yes, it may still embrace Chairman Mouse Dong's master plan to breed enough yellow-skinned bastards to fill in the Pacific Ocean and build a human invasion bridge to America's righteous shores. But at the end of the day, it's also full of motivated, highly dexterous people who represent the last, desperate trade gold mine for U.S. corporate labor exploitation. And *that* is the only reason President Bush hasn't cauterized that communism-oozing sore of a country with a few hundred tactical nukular blasts.

The Rest: American foreign policy in regard to non-Chinkonese slants is simple: Don't get in any unnecessary snits about them building atom bombs as long as the looms keep humming.

☆ Africa Policy

Your CEO knows that Africa is a nation that suffers from terrible disease. As compassionate conservatives, it behooves all White House Inc. staffers to appear that this is something that concerns them. By shedding public tears over photos of bug-eyed Africanese babies with dusty tummies swollen by maggot water, you are effectively liberated from any responsibility to care for *domestic* unfortunates—who might otherwise muster the strength to drag themselves to a polling place and vote for a Democrat.

In some regions of Africa, more than one-third of the adult population is infected with HIV. And while in America, God continues to reserve this punishment almost exclusively for homosexuals and daytime talk-show guests, you must realize that He works in mysterious ways, and as such cannot rule out His AIDS-spewing anger welling up and splashing onto groups that President Bush minds losing. That's why, back in 2003, your CEO pledged to devote $15 billion to combating the African AIDS pandemic. In the highly unlikely event any of these funds survive congressional budget wrangling, they will be dedicated exclusively to redoubling His noble efforts to replace such lunacy-inspired initiatives as "STD education" and "safe sex" with the imminently more scientific and efficacious "Out with Condoms, In with Christ!" program.

Republicans really do care about Africastan! Why, even Reverend Pat Robertson, who spits when he mentions colored folks, owns gold and diamond mines over there!

Your CEO is confident that the future relationship between Africa and American missionaries and pharmaceutical companies will be profitable for the latter two. And as U.S. petrochemical conglomerates move swiftly to secure Africa's vast and virtually untapped oil reserves, you can take comfort in the knowledge that the land-grabs of Victorian-era Europeans will look like prissy games of croquet by comparison.

☆ South America Policy

Besides Colombia, an American protectorate and cash cow for the military industry, South America is of little interest to this administration until it decides to relieve Venezuela of the messy burden of petroleum extraction. An enormous tropical jungle swarming with Marxists, exiled dictators, the mixed-heritage spawn of Nazis, and millions of near-hairless monkey peoples, South America is also a shining international symbol of how Western laissez-faire crony capitalism can catastrophically implode—and nobody wants to dwell on that. And while your CEO remains vaguely intrigued by the knowledge that toilets flush backward there, His official stance regarding South America is shaped by the old chestnut that nonwealth-producing continents comprised of predominantly liberal countries should be seen—preferably only on a map—and not heard.

☆ Australia Policy

Australia, home to the Trapp family and the eunuchs in the Vienna Boys Choir, has been a stable and dependable American ally since the end of World War II. And though the genetic makeup of nearly its entire population is that of an exiled criminal class, President Bush will nevertheless grant Australasians immunity in the forthcoming Texas-inspired World Capital Punishment Final Solution of 2007.

☆ Antarctica Policy

Antarctica is populated almost exclusively by PhDs and liberal scientists whose brains have become so severely frostbitten, they've started hallucinating a "hole" in the sky, which they call the "O" zone. While so-called prohibitions in the Antarctic Treaty of 1959, along with its amending 1991 Protocol on Environmental Protection, have temporarily thwarted President Bush from gassing up a posse of snowmobiles and slurping down every refreshing drop of their frosty ice-cap oil, Antarctica is on His list of countries that have Weapons of Mass Destruction. As such, your CEO will have a nationally televised reason for taking the whole place over when all the more balmy countries have depeted their petroleum reserves.

VII.
FAITH-BASED
GOVERNANCE

INTRODUCTION

On January 20, 2001, President George W. Bush signed Executive Order #13199, establishing the United States Department of Faith (DOF). The DOF's mission is to infuse traditional Christian values into American politics and thereby keep in check the pernicious influences of "compassion," which, when left unmonitored, destabilizes the delicate balance envisioned by our CEO's call for "compassionate conservatism."

"Sorry, Jesus couldn't be here today. But I sure can."
(Copyright © Najlah Feanny/Corbis.)

For the duration of both of George W. Bush's four-year terms, the DOF has been entrusted with disbursing millions of federal dollars to tax-exempt religious charities. In determining which organization(s) shall receive Treasury funds, the DOF does not discriminate against any particular religion, making funds available to all churches and organizations that recognize Jesus Christ as their Lord and Savior.

One day soon, no American will be able to renew a driver's license, mail a letter, or learn their ABCs in a public school without first enjoying a nice on-the-spot baptism!

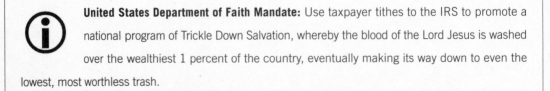

(i) **United States Department of Faith Mandate:** Use taxpayer tithes to the IRS to promote a national program of Trickle Down Salvation, whereby the blood of the Lord Jesus is washed over the wealthiest 1 percent of the country, eventually making its way down to even the lowest, most worthless trash.

UNDERSTANDING THE WORLD'S
MANY FALSE RELIGIONS

There are thousands of different faiths in the world to choose from, but the Holy Bible teaches that Christianity is the only True Religion. Therefore, you are required to classify any and all other churches or faiths as "False Religions." For your convenience, some of the most pernicious cults are listed below.

Islam: This is the official religion of terrorists. It was invented about 500 years ago by a desert-wandering camel jockey named Mohammed, who decided to make up his own religion because there was nothing like Amway in his part of the world. He wrote a book called the Koran, which tells people to worship a moon god called Allah and is filled with all sorts of strange stuff like rules for winning free virgins every time you kill a Christian and instructions for ritually disemboweling Salman Rushdie. For some weird reason no one can explain, people who practice Islam are called "Muslims," perhaps as a smokescreen for throwing CIA agents off their hummus-scented trail. These Moon Worshippers won't ever be happy, because no matter how hard they try, the closest they'll ever get to Heaven is on a Boeing 767.

Judaism: These are the people who killed Jesus. God was going to let them all into Heaven before they did that. Their book is called the Torah, Old Testament, or "Bible Without the Important Parts." It's included as part of the Bible to remind Christians what God does to things He creates that rub Him the wrong way. It also serves to underscore the fact that the Lord can be very cranky and vicious, as a harbinger of what awaits everyone when they stand before the Great White Throne of Judgment. As a corporate Christian, gainfully employed by this administration, it is your duty to honor and respect Jewish people, until the appointed time when Jesus comes back to send them all to Hell and to turn Jerusalem into the world's largest Christian Theme Park. (See "How Does Our Christian Nation Benefit by Defending Hell-Bound Jews?" — p.156)

Catholicism: These people will try to convince you that they are Christians, when in fact they are actually a Christian-*flavored* army of gold-statue-kissing, glass-bead-counting, altar-boy-humping pope lovers. Inasmuch as their blood-drinking, cannibalistic rituals, and services borrow in large, liberal doses from ancient Roman and Greek pagan rites, your employer defines Catholics as "neo-pagans." True Christians reject outright the hollow Latin nonsense spewed by their skirt-wearing priests, who run around leering at every shiny surface hoping to catch a glimpse of their false goddess Mary, who craves publicity more than her namesake Madonna. In short, to say that Catholics are Christians is a heresy tantamount to calling Senator Jeffords an American.

Buddhism: Have you ever seen a statue of a fat little bald man made out of gold while sitting in a Chinese restaurant? Well, there are some people who pray to that thing, and they're called Buddhists. Buddha was a potbellied prince who made up a religion about himself so he could sleep with anything that had two (and sometimes four!) legs. Buddhism is a religion that pretends to be simple but, in fact, is a very complicated way of sending one's self to Hell. They basically believe in thinking about nothing so hard, that they poof themselves right out of existence and drop straight down into the real God's eternal lake of fire. It is important to note that lots of Democrat Hollywood celebrity types (like Richard Gere and that llama called Dolly) claim to be Buddhists because it's popular right now.

Hinduism: Hinduism is a religion observed by people who think they become cows when they die. As a result, they won't eat McDonald's because they're afraid of getting a piece of their grandmother's vagina stuck between their teeth. Hinduism is the second most popular false religion in the world (after Islam). Hindus worship incense holders shaped like elephants and femmy-looking octopus men. Their sacred text is a pornographic coloring book called the Karma Sutra, which was written by the ugliest Beatle—George McHarrison. Though they are generally peaceful at first glance, Hindus are almost indistinguishable from terrorists. Only the nausea-inducing waves of curry breath they emit provide any level of assurance that you're not face-to-face with a bloodthirsty Muslimaniac.

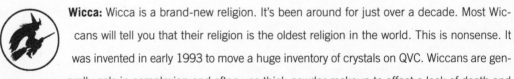

Wicca: Wicca is a brand-new religion. It's been around for just over a decade. Most Wiccans will tell you that their religion is the oldest religion in the world. This is nonsense. It was invented in early 1993 to move a huge inventory of crystals on QVC. Wiccans are generally pale in complexion and often use thick powder makeup to affect a look of death and conceal severe acne. They are given to obesity and piercing themselves and others in the nose, cheeks, eyebrows, lips, tongue, fingertips, and cervix. Wiccans are known to dress in black and congregate at Renaissance festivals, where they purchase knives, swords, and cheap earth-tone lesbian pottery from master Wiccan craftswomyn.

> **Note:** As an employee of White House Inc., in the highly unlikely event you personally should encounter a follower of a False Religion, it is your duty to witness to him. Furthermore, if you deliver someone's soul to Jesus during business hours, report the time as "SFR" on your time sheet—"Saving from a False Religion." This qualifies for time plus half.

VISITS IN THE NIGHT FROM THE PRESIDENTIAL PRAYER SQUAD

President Bush begins each weekday at the crack of nine o'clock kneeling on the floor of the Oval Office in His Batman flannel feety pajamas, holding hands with a group of Christian men. They kneel there for an hour (two hours on the Lord's Day or if there are enough doughnuts) just talking to our nation's Commander of the Commander in Chief, the Lord Jesus.

This is the Presidential Prayer Squad—an elite, patriotic force of spiritual warriors who fight on the front lines of the invisible battle between good and evil. Managed by the other holy trinity of Reverend Pat Robertson, Reverend Jerry Falwell, and Reverend Fred Phelps, the squad is made up of a rotating pool of dignified pastors, evangelists, and corporate lobbyists who have worked diligently behind the scenes for many years to get your CEO His job.

These gentlemen slayers of liberalism have free reign of the White House. They sleep, eat, and drink Jesus' financial blessings 24/7, and many of them have taken up permanent residence inside the Hall of Prayer Closets deep below the West Wing. They are also authorized to take employees into custody for any kind of interrogation they feel is necessary. This means that if you stay overnight in a guest room at the White House, and the next morning you wake up covered in polygraph sensors, strapped naked to a box spring, and look down to see Jerry Falwell using your genitals as a pincushion, you can pretty well guess that not only have you been visited in the night by the Presidential Prayer Squad, but that you may be just moments away from standing before your Lord.

THE SALVATION SECURITY ACT

Legislation Mandating Salvation of All Americans

This bill, the U.S. Department of Faith's legislative debut, is currently proceeding through the United States House of Representatives. As an employee of White House Inc., you are required to familiarize yourself with the Bill's goals and content.

United States Department of Faith, Salvation Legislation Bill
Public Summary, United States Congress

Title: The Salvation Security Act is a bill intended to save all natural-born or natu-ralized Americans (unless they are Mexicans who snuck in and are, therefore, exempt from honoring immigration laws applicable to everyone else) (hereinafter "Real Ameri-cans") from the eternal fires of certain damnation at the hands of the Lord who loves them (hereinafter "SS Act"). The SS Act will allow Congress to monitor, catalogue, and track all Real Americans who fail to attend churches that patriotically honor the Bible-believing principles upon which the United States of America was founded or other-wise, by omission or commission, fail to sufficiently flatter the Lord Jesus Christ to the point thereby that it is a legal certainty (provable in a court of law using the "preponderance of the evidence" not "beyond a reasonable doubt" standard) that the Lord Jesus will throw said Real American into the sulfurous pits of an everlasting Hell (hereinafter "Deserved Destiny").

Preamble: Being so that it is perfectly clear that religious zealots (of the non-Christian persuasion) were allowed to attack America on September 11, 2001, because the previous non-Christian administration was too busy being orally pleasured by sundry hussies and harlots, thereby allowing non-Christians in every conceivable position of power (whether under the Oval Office desk or elsewhere) to propagate a national illu-sion of secular security obtained without the active or willing assistance of anyone living in the sky (hereinafter "Godless State"). It is a historical fact that the United States was founded on Bible-based Christian principles, including, but not lim-ited to, a loathing of witches, and all recent causes of unrest, death, and downward stock prices have and are being caused by a gloating, homosexual tap dancer named Lucifer made bold by said rejection and/or neglect of those Godly principles. It is hereby noted that a mandatory and immediate return to those Christian principles prac-ticed by our Founding Fathers (hereinafter "Puritans") should be the nation's most urgent priority.

Section 1: The United States Department of Faith shall use each decennial census to catalog and record Real Americans who neglect to use a No. 2 pencil to fill in the cir-cle next to "Bible-Believing Christian" as their religion. This information shall within sixty days of completion of said applicable census be fed by Scantron into the National Law Enforcement Database, and the list of all Americans who have, in the stated manner, failed to exhibit sufficient faith to entitle them to salvation shall be made available to all municipal and city police departments, employers, restaurants, and department stores (this list shall hereinafter be referred to as "Unsaved").

Section 2: The Department of Faith will use $8 billion, said funds previously squandered on keeping old people breathing long after they are either attractive or useful, to work with local pastors and Christian police officers to monitor, approach, and inform these Unsaved of the forty-five-day (from the date of ratification of the SS Act, to be extended if the last day falls on a bank holiday, but NOT on a Sunday) grace period in which to repent, fall to their knees, and accept Jesus Christ as their Lord and Savior (hereinafter "Grace Period"). This Grace Period shall be tolled if Unsaved falls into a religious trance, coma, or otherwise becomes medically without the capacity to think. Conclusive and irrefutable evidence of an inability to think shall be the joining of one of the following cults: Jehovah's Witness, Scientology, Latter-day Saints, Branch Davidians, or MoveOn.org.

Section 3: Once the Grace Period for repentance has expired, the Unsaved will be given ten business days to relocate to a country that doesn't mind having its values spit upon. During the ten-day relocation period, the Unsaved's assets will be frozen and their bank and investment accounts and credit limit(s) on Visa, MasterCard, American Express, Diners Club, and Discover (hereinafter "Unsaved Savings") will be reduced to a cumulative total of $200 or the value of a Greyhound one-way bus ticket to Canada or Mexico, whichever is less. After the ten-day relocation period, Unsaved Savings will be transferred to the Department of Faith to defray the costs of erecting clothed likenesses of the Lord Jesus Christ holding a sexagonal red "Stop and Pray" sign on every intersection in America. Any Unsaved identified by bar-code tattoo scan, or simply a phone call from a concerned neighbor or passing car, will be dealt with as seen fit within the unbridled discretion of the Attorney General to have them put down or otherwise inconvenienced. As matters of national security are deemed ipso facto to be involved in such cases, issues of the so-called cruelness or even unusualness of any chosen punishment shall be wholly irrelevant. Further, it shall be recognized by any court of competent jurisdiction that, as a matter of law, any such objection will only be raised by those who are a present and certain security risk to our nation and all who love her and are in need of a minimum jail sentence of no less than fifteen years.

Section 4: The President of the United States will have the right to deploy the National Guard, Army, Navy, Marines, Air Force, CIA, or other operatives too secret to mention herein (hereinafter collectively referred to as "Enforcers") in the event that this bill cannot be peacefully enforced, but such deployment must be ratified by two-thirds of the Presidential Prayer Team within ten days of deployment or the Enforcers must be withdrawn within 135 days (said 135 days may be extended by a public or nonpublic Executive Order).

Section 5: This bill will be effective immediately. Unsaved are hereby notified that America has reloaded and Unsaved have fifty-five days to be in a country that doesn't mind harboring atheistic scum. Unsaved are also reminded that while there is a slim chance that they may evade the jurisdiction of American courts, they shall not avoid being called before the White Throne of Judgment, before which they shall have no right to an attorney or even a drink of water.

HOW DOES OUR CHRISTIAN NATION BENEFIT BY DEFENDING HELL-BOUND JEWS?

As America approaches the final days before the Lord Jesus' return, one of the questions asked most often by new White House Inc. employees is, "Why does our Christian nation support a country like Israel, when its population is responsible for the death of our savior?" Should someone ask you this, simply reply, "Read your Bible!" That's a good answer, and a solid piece of advice, too. In fact, your CEO recommends that all employees cancel their subscriptions to *The Washington Post* and turn instead to His favorite morning-headline source, the book of Revelation, which spells out in explicit detail the End Times events that are at this very moment unfolding across the globe.

> *It might be difficult for you to feign love for those who were responsible for both Woody Allen and killing your savior, but doesn't knowing how their story is going to end make it easier to play along?*

It is a fact that one of the many reasons that America is so much more blessed than the cesspool of rancid, filthy, non–English-speaking so-called countries that make up the rest of this world is that its government has always supported the nation of Israel. Sadly, it was often for all the wrong, secular, and liberal-minded reasons—like goyim genocide guilt and so-called international humanitarian decency. But as a True Christian, President Bush knows the *real* reason is that America is bound to obey Genesis 12:3, and to bless the unsaved Jews as a race and a nation. In return, we Christians alone will be rewarded with eternal bliss in the hereafter.

☆ **No doubt many Jews will be shocked in the last days to hear Jesus bellow "CHECK-MATE!" as the clouds part and He descends upon Jerusalem to unleash a bloodbath of unimaginable ferocity. Well they shouldn't be.**

The President would like you to know that since the nation of Israel was restored in 1948, Christian leaders and Republican National Committee operatives have been working round the clock to get 144,000 Jews to accept Christ as their Lord and Savior. This might seem like a small goal, but they are a mighty willful bunch. Once that number is hit, the Apocalypse can begin with a flourish (Revelation 7:2–4) and Jesus will return to kill off everyone who doesn't have a little statue of him hanging from the rearview mirror of his Chevy Suburban. Fortunately, that means most of Real America is safe.

🙏 Official 🙏 Employee Prayer

1. I admit that I was powerless before joining White House Inc. My life prior to employment by George W. Bush was without worth and unmanageable.

2. I have come to believe that my employment here has restored me to sanity and liquidity.

3. I have made a decision to turn my life over to the care of the Republican Party and the eternal grace of President Bush. I vow on the pretax inheritance from my father to serve the President until my use to Him is wrung dry, and I am summarily cast aside like a fabricated justification for a politically expedient war.

4. I have scoured my past history and turned over a written moral inventory as comprehensive and incriminating as any homosexual actor's Scientology file.

5. I have confessed any previous wrongdoings to my company-appointed pastor and to the beautiful Main Hall oil portrait of my Personal Savior, George W. Bush.

6. My orientation interrogation was uncontrived, and all of my degrading secrets divulged therein are now a matter of corporate record, with their potentially humiliating dissemination solely in the righteous hands of my employer.

7. Any of my character shortcomings that could not be dealt with through medication have now been harnessed and cultivated so that I may better serve the Party in ways unimaginable to those cruelly hampered by scruples.

8. I have submitted a list of every person with whom I will share the empowering, angry doctrines of neoconservatism. I promise to contact them during nonworking hours and witness diligently to collect their souls.

9. Should I encounter resistance from friends who are lost to the unseemly empathy of liberalism, they shall become dead to me, and I will report them to authorities enforcing the Salvation Security Act.*

10. I will commune daily with my immediate supervisor to divulge, before a stenographer, any new, embarrassing personal information that might otherwise have remained private for the duration of my gainful employment.

11. I will read my King James Bible daily and participate with dutiful awe and supplication in mandatory morning prayers, animal sacrifices, and semihourly Bible-study sessions.

12. I am overjoyed to be a part of this noble corporation, and promise to carry the message of sublime entitlement through pure and absolute obedience to the Republican Party, Jesus Christ, and the first True Christian President, the Great George Walker Bush.

*See p. 154.

VIII.
INSIDE THE
WEST WING

It is not for kings, O Lemuel—
not for kings to drink wine,
not for rulers to crave beer,
lest they drink and forget what the law decrees,
and deprive all the oppressed of their rights.

—Proverbs 31:4–5

WORKING WITH PRESIDENT BUSH

President Bush's semiconspicuous lack of hands-on engagement, coupled with a passionate disinclination to read or ask questions, should in no way be misinterpreted to mean that His job is not getting done. Quite the contrary: someone is doing your CEO's job at all times, leaving Him free to attend to raising roomfuls of campaign cash.

Consider yourself a privileged worker indeed if your job here at White House Inc. is based in the West Wing. These posts are the most coveted in all of government and involve close contact with our CEO during those scant hours of the month when He is not at the Western White House, Camp David, or sitting cross-legged on the family quarters floor eating Jiffy Pop and playing Xbox. This section contains the valuable additional information you'll need to do your job well.

☆ **WEST WING WORKING TIP: Because you may find yourself within mere feet of the CEO at any given time, you should always remove your shoes and speak only in whispers. Otherwise, you might interrupt a restorative presidential nap and subject all of your coworkers to the wrath of a cranky boss!**

THE ART OF DELEGATING DELEGATION

Immediately after His election as America's first-ever CEO President, George W. Bush wasted no time establishing an all-new, *corporate-based* White House culture, replete with traditional attire (see Dress Code—p. 63)

 Rules to Work by: When in the presence of the President, always remember:

1. Never speak unless spoken to.
2. Use only approved titles: Mr. President, Governor, Your Highness, Chief, El Jefe, or Massah Bush.
3. You are never too busy to join the President for a tension-busting round of patty-cake, Don't Flinch, or Smear the Queer.

and an indefatigable commitment to creative accounting. Central to this effort was the wholehearted embracing of the hallowed management concept of "delegation"—a time-honored method for those of consequence to rightfully bypass the results-impeding tedium of actual work in favor of passing the buck to anonymous underlings better suited for accountability and white-collar incarceration.

As a capitalist superman visionary, our CEO has taken this concept to its logical conclusion: the wholesale delegation of delegation. In late January 2001, President Bush executed a flawless, one-time delegation of the delegation of all distracting minutiae required to operate the Executive Branch to Vice President Richard B. Cheney. Once unburdened thusly, the President was better able to attend to the many pressing matters befitting someone of His stature—so that even if evil Arabs are flying American jets into buildings in New York while Mr. Bush is listening to a children's story in a Florida classroom, the inconvenience of terrorism need not prevent Him from hearing what happened to that cute little pet goat!

☆ **TIP: If a task is delegated to you, you in turn should redelegate it to a subordinate, who will do the same. Eventually, said task is delegated into oblivion, thereby freeing anyone from bearing responsibility—except for the Democratic Party, of course, which, as we all know, fucks everything up and is to blame for every social plague since before the founding of the Masons.**

Winners Come Prepared

Whether in a formal Roosevelt Room meeting or a convivial men's room trough-urinal chat, each exchange with your CEO can be an important opportunity to reaffirm your grasp on the issues and see if you measure up. So if you're truly serious about ascending up the White House Inc. ladder to luxury and untold riches, you'll make it a point to always have memorized the latest issues of *Runner's World* and *The Family Circus*, lest you find yourself unprepared for a rapid-fire presidential quiz on shock-dampening ratings of Saucony arch-support systems, prevailing chafing ointment formulations—or the latest knee-slapping antics of Jeffy and PJ.

THE FOLKSY CHARM OF SARCASTIC NICKNAMES AND INSULTS

Our CEO's down-home warmth is legendary. Anyone who's ever known or worked with Him consistently remarks on His seemingly preternatural ability to break through the walls of formality with His signature brand of unguarded charm. A veritable fountain of affability, even to folks who don't matter, the President excels at making people feel welcome and valued through the spirited hurling of endearing, sarcastic insults and derisive nicknames.

Nicknames

The list is long: Pootie Poot, Chrome Dome, Numbnuts, Bitchy the Snatch, and many more (see p. 163). As a White House Inc. staffer, you'll soon have a nickname of your own, too. Delivered when you least expect it with an impish, bile-filled smirk, not only does your new presidential handle mean you've made your triumphant debut on our CEO's passive-aggressive radar screen, it will also serve as your personal password to the VIP locker-room sauna.

You know, if you are quick with a rib-tickler or a personal comeback like I am, you can breeze right through an annual press conference without answering a single question. All anyone remembers is what a swell fellow you are and how much fun you must have been back in the days when you used to slip off your skivvies and wag your dick on top of the frat-house bar!

Presidential Nicknames of Note

A working knowledge of the President's lexicon of affectionate monikers is essential to understanding His orders. As such, all West Wing employees are required to memorize the list below. Note also that addenda to this directory are posted to the intranet each Tuesday afternoon.

DOMESTIC FIGURES

- Laura Bush: "Pickles"
- Jeb Bush: "Gator"
- Dick Cheney: "Mr. Cheney, Sir"
- Wesley Clark: "General Leslie Skidmark"
- Bill Clinton: "Fat Chick Fucker"
- Hilly Clinton: "Senator Carpetbaggermuncher"
- Tom Daschle: "Asshole"
- Howard Dean: "Jughead"
- Tom DeLay: "Roach Motel"
- Barney Frank: "Fruit Loop"
- Dick Gephardt: "Lady-brows"

    NOTE: When together, Gephardt and Frank are known as "Blondie and Fagwood"

- Ruth Bader Ginsburg: "Lezzie the 4-Eyes"
- Al Gore: "Mr. Poopy-Pants-Loser-Dickhead-Sucker"
- Katharine Harris: "Avon Lady"
- Dennis Hastert: "Penis Hastahurt"
- Charlton Heston: "Grandpa Moses"
- Karen Hughes: "Butch"
- Ted Kennedy: "Lifeguard"
- John Kerry: "Lurch"
- Henry Kissinger: "Jewboy Classic"
- Kenneth Lay: formerly "Kenny Boy," but now "That Guy Everyone Yaps About"
- Joe Lieberman: "Jewboy 2000"
- Rush Limbaugh: "Little Blues"
- Trent Lott: "Dippity-Do"
- Mary Matalin: "Houdini"

- Ralph Nader: "Jackpot"

- Peggy Noonan: "Shakespeare"

- Oliver North: "Colonel Mum's-the-Word"

- Colin Powell: "Boy"

- William Rehnquist: "Leader of the Pack"

- Ralph Reed: "Kid Klinefelter"

- Condi Rice: "Tar Babe"

- Karl Rove: "Mr. President"

- Donald Rumsfeld: "Duke Nukem"

- Antonin Scalia: "Pitbull the Dago"

- Arnold Schwarzenegger: "Adolf Shriverbanger"

- David Souter: "Daddy's Little Traitor"

- Jimmy Swaggart: "Motel 6"

- Clarence Thomas: "Long Dong Slivva"

- Oprah Winfrey: "Chocosaurus"

FOREIGN FIGURES

- Bertie Ahern: "Potato McDrunky"

- Kofi Annan: "Buckwheat"

- Yasser Arafat: "Picnic Basket Head"

- Silvio Berlusconi: "Garlicko"

- Osama bin Laden: "Saddam Hussein"

- Tony Blair: "My Bee-otch"

- Jacques Chirac: "Froggy le Poodle"

- Jean Chretien: "Governor 51"

- Kim Jong-Il: "Dog Breath"

- Tayyip Erdogan: "Butterball"

- Pablo Escobar: "Candy Man"

- Vicente Fox: "Frito Bandito"

- Tarja Halonen: "Who?"

- John Howard: "Dingo-Berry"

- Saddam Hussein: "Osama bin Laden"

- Hamid Karzai: "Pinocchio"

- Ayatollah Khamenei: "Ass-a-hola Cockamamie"

- Junichiro Koizumi: "Chopstix"

- Aleksander Kwasniewski: "Kaiser Kielbasa"

- Hosni Mubarak: "Pharaoh Hos-Mu"

- Pervez Musharraf: "The Pervertster"

- Pope John Paul II: "Hunchy the Popo"

- Vladimir Putin: "Pooty Poot"

- Muammar al-Qadhafi: "Momo al-Labia"

- Prince Abdullah Saud: "Your Royal Highness Prince Abdullah Saud, Sir"

- Gerhard Schröder: "Herr Gerschtrapo"

- Ariel Sharon: "Shlomo Psychostein"

- Jiang Zemin: "Jiang, Jiang, Chicken Wiang"

Insults

Our CEO stresses often that our jobs here at White House Inc. are just that—jobs. That's why, while it may be tempting to overwork or invest ourselves emotionally in the thankless grind of our nine-to-five duties, President Bush never misses an opportunity to put things in perspective by introducing a healthy dose of irreverent levity. So the next time you find yourself self-importantly delivering another long, boring, and gratuitously complicated Cabinet Room PowerPoint presentation, don't be surprised to hear the President playfully prick your officiousness with a knowingly wry, "What a total asshole!" or "That was so interesting I forgot to think, butthole-breath!"

☆ **TIP: In the rough-and-tumble world of Washington, D.C., politics, nobody gets mad—they get even. As a White House Inc. employee, you must strive to cultivate the ability to smile and chirp, "Great to see ya, pardner!" when you're really thinking, "Why don't you eat shit and die, you slimy, walrus-looking fuck?"**

PHOTO-OP PROTOCOLS

The life of today's average American is hectic. Between shoveling down drive-through meals in the SUV and squeezing in one's requisite seven-hour allotment of reality TV, who's got time to lounge around *reading* like some liberal? Americans prefer to receive their presidential performance reports in blink-of-an-eye-short, candy-sweet visual nuggets. Our CEO understands this, which is why White House Inc. has taken great pains to elevate the once-humdrum photo op to a veritable art form.

President Bush prefers Estée Lauder Double Matte Oil-Control Powder. (Copyright © Brooks Kraft/Corbis.)

As a staffer, you will be called upon to assist in the production of these meticulously crafted facsimiles of spontaneous, patriotic sincerity. Please make note of your duties for each type of photo op below.

Type I: Aircraft Carriers—When preventing a few thousand war-weary sailors' months-overdue homecoming in order to stage a campaign event on their vessel's deck, always have the captain turn the ship around—lest the clear, starboard-side view of boardwalk hot-dog vendors or gyrating wharf hookers shatter the illusion of high-seas bravery. Also, NEVER attempt to assist the President while He is elbow deep in His flight suit arranging tube socks around the first giblets.

MISSION ACCOMPLISHED
OPERATION BULGING CODPIECE

Type II: Disaster Scenes—Once a scene has been declared safe enough to walk through in dress shoes, quickly locate a photo setting that adequately captures the sheer telegenic horror of the disaster. If this is not possible, enhance your shoot with dramatic smoke by jamming a roll of whiskey-soaked toilet paper in an old coffee can, then igniting the makeshift smelter just off-camera. NOTE: Should dangerous conditions mandate a flyover instead of an on-site visit, simply distribute any file photo of an indigestion-ravaged President Bush grimacing out of his Air Force One window.

"Them poor folks look even more like ants from up here!"

Type III: Colored Children—Nothing stimulates the illusion of inclusiveness like flanking the President with a small herd of carefully screened and dipped pickaninnies. Note, however, that such occasions call for the strict enforcement of the following rules: all boom boxes checked at the door, afros "conked," shoes tied (no "high-tops"), and no speaking except for succinct, non-Ebonics sound bites disparaging affirmative action. Also, note that all the little photo models are subject to search for stolen hubcaps, silverware, and small objets d'art prior to departing the White House grounds.

Still photography is recommended for all such thirty-second events.

"Makes you wonder how big their penis wrinkles are!"

Type IV: Mount Rushmore—On a clear day, South Dakota's Mount Rushmore makes for a majestic and versatile photo backdrop. The patriotic play of natural light and shadows off the noble profiles of dead white men serves to distractingly complement presidential announcements heralding the discontinuation of so-called social programs and civil liberties. NOTE: After erecting the presidential podium, be certain to position the photographer's pool at just the right angle so that in all photos, it will be all but impossible to include (supposedly) Republican Abraham Lincoln's conceited federalist smirk.

Type V: The Crawford "Ranch"—It is very important to maintain *multiple* photo-op locations at the Western White House, lest Americans see the same setting too many times and realize that the President spends four months a year kicking it in Texas instead of actually working at His Washington, D.C., office. Therefore, carefully select a new plot of fire ant–infested prairie every other week, taking special care to ensure as many of the following appear in the hardscrabble background: three (or more) bales of hay, two longhorn steer, and one picturesquely dilapidated slave shack. The Mexican gardeners in Crawford are instructed to plant mature camera-ready brush one week before the President's arrival so that He can spend five minutes clearing it to the delight of throngs of AP and evening-news cameramen.

Outdoor klieg lighting helps accent cedar sap smudges.

Type VI: Poor People—As part of our ongoing efforts to convince 51 percent of the population to vote for an agenda carefully designed to benefit 1 percent, it is sometimes necessary for the President to be photographed fraternizing with the Other Classes. Whether that means touring a family farm or simply marveling at a cutting-edge Piggly Wiggly checkout scanner, just know that it is your responsibility to provide the President with a fresh antibacterial Handi Wipe in the unlikely event He is touched by some filthy, naked, piss-poor-inbred-snot-dripping toddler.

Type VII: Bill Signings—Photographs of public bill signings make for compelling evidence that not only is the President forging boldly ahead to enact the right-wing legislative agenda of a handful of His superiors, but more important, that, contrary to vicious liberal rumors, He is functionally literate. In warm weather, these photo ops are held in the Rose Garden. During winter months, either the East Room or Cross Hall is a fitting setting. Your job is to ensure that—regardless of whether the President will be seated—no Democrats or Republicans over 5'10" are permitted within a twenty-foot radius while tape is rolling or shutters are snapping.

Type VIII: Heads of State Visits—Our CEO is determined to demonstrate America's commitment to engaging in all global affairs that impact the quarterly earnings statements of Halliburton, the Carlyle Group, ExxonMobil, and Chevron-Texaco. As such, He proudly makes it a point to reward any and all world leaders who genuflect before Him (although Tony Blair's chummy habit of sneaking into the President's bed when everyone else has gone to sleep should *not* be emulated by non-British envoys) with a coveted daylong photo op at His Texas home. On such occasions, be aware that beyond the

With Japanese prime minister Junichiro Koizumi.

With Benito Murdoch.

routine Crawford protocols (see Type V, above), you are also responsible for confiscating film from any photographers not adhering to the "NEVER document the President cracking up at funny-talking foreigners" edict.

(i)   **Backdrop Guidelines:** To help a public whose attention tends to wander after a sentence or two if you do anything other than kidnap a photogenic white female, all White House Inc. personnel are forbidden to appear before a working camera without first reporting to the Decorative Propaganda Team. Upon giving Karl Rove the two-word gist of your speech, you will be provided with a television-friendly, "on message" backdrop that endlessly repeats a pithy slogan summing up what your speech should be about even if it isn't. The "Mission Accomplished" backdrop is our most popular, having

been used with great success for everything from the commemoration of the start of anarchy in Iraq to condolences for Senator Wellstone's death. It must be booked two weeks in advance. Since these screens contain the only words from your speech that voters will remember, they free you up to devote your entire speech to a random collection of preapproved patriotic stories about blue-collar Americans you've never met, but with whom you can pretend to empathize.

"Fool me once. . . don't get fooled again!"

CARING FOR CORPORATE FRIENDS

You should always keep in mind that during your near-constant interaction with the titans of the international business community—whether by mail, e-mail, telephone, letter, or from a sexually submissive vantage point on a vibrating Motel 6 bed—you are representing White House Inc., and as such should take pains to conduct yourself properly. You should be courteous, strike an appropriately sycophantic tone, and avoid making any statements that might shake our Corporate Friends' confidence in our ability to do their bidding.

When Jesus said that it is easier for a camel to go through the eye of a needle than it is for a rich man to enter the kingdom of Heaven, He left out important details, like what if the needle is ten stories tall?

Whatever you do, never feel guilty for representing the President's tight dodgeball circle of business partners to the exclusion of all others. By doing unto the Holy 1 percent as you would have them do unto you, you are merely demonstrating true friendship. And friends share their toys—whether it be a classic Buck Rogers Rocket Pistol or a few billion in federal funds ripe for diverting into the sandbox of a corporate warlord's state-level fiefdom.

Friends also remember favors, and they don't snitch on each other or forget to shred each other's memos. In short, friends are there for you when you need them most—like when you get caught with a dead whore in the trunk of your Bimmer, or when pesky congressmen start nosing around into how everyone in Texas got so rich while driving California bankrupt.

Use the following guidelines to help ensure that our valuable relationships with the Ayn Rand worshipping titans of global industry and finance remain not only intact, but strong and vibrant:

⭐ **DO'S:**

- Maintain decorum. Never address a Corporate Friend by his first name. Always refer to him as "Mr. [Insert Family Name Here] or simply "Master."

- When entertaining your Corporate Friend, keep an ample supply of cigars and cognac on hand at all times (but never mention they come from Cuba or France if you don't want something warm and brown spat in your face).

- Be certain to supply your home telephone number to your assigned Corporate Friend(s). He may need something in the middle of the night!

- Demonstrate conspicuous commitment: Holding your arm over a liquid-fuel blowtorch—G. Gordon Liddy style—is a wonderful way to express your obedience.

- After making a new Corporate Friend, be sure to add him to the following White House Inc. official lists: Backstage All-Access, Christmas Card, and Trust-Buster-Buster.

🚫 **DON'TS:**

- NEVER save documents. While it's natural to want to collect hot and steamy love letters in your personal life, their political equivalents must always be promptly incinerated.

- Do not play hard to get with any Corporate Friend. Instead, revel in the gloriousness of his skeletal embrace and breath-stealing kisses.

- Avoid interrupting your Corporate Friend while he is gorging at the trough your political connections have allowed you to shove under his grateful snout.

PROCESSING SUBJECTIVE INTELLIGENCE

Inasmuch as America is the richest, handsomest, most popular alpha male at school, the United States has many enemies who are jealous that we get to screw all the cute countries, so we must rule the global playground with an iron fist. A steady stream of intelligence on all foreign cliques of losers and spazmos is an essential component of maintaining our righteous stranglehold on the rest of the world. As a White House Inc. employee, should your duties include assisting in the analysis of the reams of intelligence data we receive each day, you should adhere to the guidelines set forth below:

1. **Prioritization:** Do not allow minor issues to distract you from *important* intelligence matters. For instance, should a despised, saxophone-playing political rival launch America's cruise missiles against our most dangerous foe, deride his foolish efforts as a shameless attempt to interrupt your monomaniacal fixation on his penis. Then, later, mock him for not having leveled more aspirin factories than he did.

2. **Focus Groups:** Ascertain which issues—aside from "cheap gas" and "more money and stuff for me"—resonate best with voters. Find out what types of people they hate and want to see publicly crucified. To do so, randomly assemble well-rounded focus groups from such bastions of diversity as monster-truck rallies; Branson, Missouri, concerts; and Las Vegas defense contractor conferences.

3. **Figurehead Identification:** When confronted with a ballooning global movement of extremely violent religious zealots, focus all energies into demonizing one easily identifiable Iraqi figurehead without regard to his actual importance. Follow up by allowing him to elude capture for years on end, thereby stoking the election-friendly fires of domestic paranoia (see Terrorism—p. 100).

4. **Knowing Whom to Ignore:** When forced to decide between conflicting interpretations of sensitive, potentially lifesaving intelligence data, it is critical to consider the source. Ask yourself, which FBI, CIA, and/or NSA agents can be counted on to produce intelligence that doesn't impudently undermine the company's political objectives? And of those, who will clam up when the allegations our CEO publicly attributes to him turn out to contradict his actual findings?

5. **Determining Imminent Threat:** When scrutinizing intelligence to decide whether or not America faces a greater threat from, say, an aggressive and nuclear-capable Oriental with Don King hair, or a hobbled and defenseless Arabiac with a Magnum, P.I., mustache, it is useful to ask yourself the following questions to assess the menace of each evildoer:

- Has he personally made the President's daddy look like a sissy?

- Has he personally tried to assassinate the President's daddy?

- Has he personally inflicted financial harm upon the President's daddy by damaging or destroying—whether actively or via neglect—valuable petrochemical equipment and products?

RESPONDING TO TREASONOUS BIPARTISAN CRITICISM

 While most of President Bush's tenure has been marked by complete and total GOP supremacy, it is essential we keep our debating foils sharp—lest complacency about other people's ideas prove our collective undoing. Below are various sample criticisms you may encounter if you ever venture beyond your neoconservative covey of friends—or *The Washington Times* editorial page. Each startlingly rude question is followed by a devastating retort preferred by today's most gifted conservative polemicists. You are encouraged to study and emulate these exchanges carefully—and remember that only a fool ventures "off message" and inserts his real thoughts, ideas, and observations.

Them: In the wake of 9/11, the Bush Administration's doctrine of unilateralist preemptive strikes has contributed to a dangerous escalation in global anti-Americanism.

You: Bill Clinton got his dick sucked by that fat chick!

Them: Despite an avowed commitment to fiscal responsibility, President Bush's economic policies have single-handedly spawned the most massive budget deficit in our nation's history.

You: At least George W. Bush can keep his cock in his pants, liberal traitor!

Them: By dismissing criticisms of his economic policies as attempts to spark "class warfare," isn't President Bush merely deploying a blatant smokescreen to conceal the fact that the only *significant* tax cuts he's granting are to multimillionaires in the ultra-yacht and Learjet crowd?

You: Clearly you'd be happier with a *Hummer-Getter* in the *Blow-val* Office, Dummycrat!

Them: By manipulating intelligence to falsely suggest Iraq was an imminent threat, President Bush recklessly stretched our military paper-thin and sent hundreds of soldiers to their deaths for no other reason than to seize oil fields and settle a personal, familial score.

You: At least Dubya's missiles are kicking dirty Muslimiac ass, not poking fat, Jewish cakehole, you Sore-Loserman Tree-Hugger!

☆ **Fun Tip:** Whenever vocalizing an idea or assertion that is so preposterous as to be laughable, take a page from former Press Secretary Ari Fleischer's playbook and precede your statement with "The American people understand that . . ." Try taking it for a spin on the following phrases:

☞ The American people understand that even if you're a middle-class nobody, you'll reap the benefits of massive tax cuts designed for Bill Gates.

☞ The American people understand that it makes sense to strengthen Social Security by emulating the best practices of our nation's fiscally steady and impeccably scrupulous mega offshore shell corporations.

☞ The American people understand that free health care is inferior in all those other countries where people have much longer life expectancies than we do.

☞ The American people understand that the President is entitled to four months of vacation every year, as, thanks to the President's Trickle Down Economy, many of them are now enjoying twelve-month vacations from work.

THE UNITED STATES SECRET SERVICE

"Three out of 43 ain't bad."—Secret Service Motto

By now, you've no doubt noticed the phalanx of what would appear to be hunky, heavily armed funeral directors flanking our CEO at all times. These are Secret Service agents, and they are responsible for ensuring the safety of the President, the Vice President, and their codependents. And while guarding the two most powerful and morally exceptional people on the face of the Earth is a tough job, it's one these gentlemen handle with fabled aplomb. As a White House Inc. employee, it behooves you to understand the duties of these omnipresent, Ray-Ban–wearing centurions.

? Frequently Asked Employee Questions About the United States Secret Service

Q: What kind of guns do Secret Service agents carry?

Boy howdy, somebody makes a move on POTUS—hell, even on one of His yappy-assed dogs—and it's the Iraqi Highway of Death all over again—charred ragheads dead on their knees holding piles of ashes that were once their own stinking guts. I was in the S-H-I-T! Anyone wants to get down and boogie, I'M READY TO FUCKING DANCE!

A: That information is classified. You need only know that whatever they've got, it's enough to get the job done. They may or may not have bulletproof briefcases with concealed MAC-10s in them. Or they may or may not have two 9mms strapped under each arm, a locked and loaded TEC-9 down each trouser leg, and even a couple .22 snub-noses Velcroed up behind their nutsacks—right there on the man taint.

Q: Does the Secret Service investigate *every* threat against the President?

A: Yes. The law requires thorough investigation of all threats made against the President—be they written, verbal, or simply an errant thought by an otherwise suspicious person. If a threat appears genuine, the offender is terminated with extreme prejudice. Also note that the definition of "threat" has been recently expanded to include the following: protesting; political cartooning; not saving the President's

Special Agent Burt Johnson

speeches on TiVo; the writing of tell-all books by cheap, bottle-blonde ex-sisters-in-law; and generally sub-verting the GOP agenda—even if only at the water cooler.

Q: How close can a suspected threat—be he Arab or environmentalist—get to the White House before the Secret Service can dispatch him?

A: While it technically depends on when the rooftop 25-mm Gatling cannon's targeting computer first gets a solid lock, 1.4 miles is generally as close as anyone can get unless they are disguised as a Saudi trillion-aire. At that point, the threat-neutralization process is not unlike liquefying civilian-impersonating Afghans or Iraqazoids from the skids of a Black Hawk chopper. On a related note, liberal and foreign brains are not entirely dissimilar to egg yolks. When a kiwi-size round hits a suspect's head, the pop will top and FLING—yolk's flying all over your pink Chanel suit and matching pillbox hat. Only it isn't yellow. It's more like oat-meal. With little pieces of worms in it.

Q: What are the qualifications to become a Secret Service agent?

A: Most agents emerge from the ranks of U.S. Special Forces or some similar paramili tary law-enforcement unit that the Constitution is graciously vague about preventing. They must also be male, hung like a grizzly, have excellent vision and reflexes, and generally represent a perfect fusion of a True Patriot, the Terminator, and a *Guns & Ammo*–subscribing survivalist.

> *When I was Vice President, Bar was always checking in with the Secret Service guys to see if any jobs had opened up that day that could advance my career. And the fact that my son Neil was scheduled to have John Hinckley, Jr.'s brother over to his home the same week John tried to kill off my boss Ronnie (as was rudely revealed by the tattletales at The Houston Post on March 31, 1981) had no more to do with a Bush attempting to become president absent a vote than my other son Jeb having that Katharine Harris gal over for purely social reasons!*

Q: POTUS, FLOTUS—these are special code names for the President and the First Lady. Do regular employees have code names too?

A. Yes. Bullet Sponges.

IX.
INSIDE THE
EAST WING

From the Saddle of
Mrs. George W. Bush

Dear New Employee,

Welcome to the club! If you're a cheerful person like me who never complains, you will thoroughly enjoy working at whatever drudgery is required in my hubby's administration. Heavens to Betsy, you will find, after a while, that you never even think about your lack of privacy or candor. You will come to almost regard authenticity as a burden, gladly shed for the greater good.

As you know, I am rarely allowed to communicate with anyone who isn't a fidgeting five-year-old with a coloring book and an afro full of lice. That's why I am so delighted to be able to write to you and tell you what an honor it is to work on Bushie's behalf and recite the inspiringly uncontroversial pleasantries his handlers have thoughtfully chosen for us to repeat with diligent frequency every day.

Of course, you may find that making the White House your home away from home takes some adjustment. After all, we traditionally think of home as a place where you can pull down the shades, fire up the blender, and escape from all of those nagging, curious people always wanting to know why you are crying or ripping through old photographs. Not that I'm complaining, but sharing this rambling, drafty two-story warehouse of Jackie Kennedy bric-a-brac with hundreds of loud, strange men is nobody but a Reno hooker's idea of "home sweet home."

Oh, but I can be such a silly billy sometimes! Dear me, if I were actually with you, I would hug your neck right now. Of course, if you pass me in the hall and I ignore you—or even snap or snarl—just remember that we all have our own crosses to bear and it isn't fair to judge what others may be going through. So again, welcome—or as our Mexican field hands back in Texas might say in that quaintly vowel-rich language of theirs, "Mi Casa Blanco, Su Casa Blanco!"

Sincerely,

Lau

Mrs. George W. Bush (Laura)

ATTENDING TO OUR NATION'S FIRST LADY

As President Bush is fond of telling every visiting head of state when his lovely wife walks in late for a diplomatic dinner: "Brother, it sure takes a lot to take that show on the road!" Indeed, Mrs. Bush requires scores of assistants to fulfill her official duties as the submissive, silent, passive-aggressive wife every real American man strives to have in the kitchen. So whether your assigned task is to select a bulge-concealing poly-blend untailored jacket from Sears, or to pick up broken porcelain and upturned chairs and tables in the First Lady's wake, our corporate goal is to make Mrs. Bush look good. If she doesn't look good, people get fired.

☆ **TIP: If the goal of making the First Lady appear presentable in public does not seem humanly or chemically possible at any given time, you are simply to notify the press that Mrs. Bush has gone hiking with a pack of her effusively feminine, heterosexual girlfriends and is unavailable for photographs or interviews until further notice.**

The First Lady's Wardrobe

If you are serving as one of the First Lady's wardrobe attendants, you will oversee the acquiring, patching, and postholiday augmenting with elasticized panels of garments that help crystallize Mrs. Bush's wholesome and feminine image as a Republican housewife who is so busy talking about her remote youth teaching, she never has time to shop. You will also be responsible for orchestrating makeup illusions that draw attention away from a Donny Osmond haircut and chain-smoker's vertical lip crevasses on scale with a shar-pei's back folds.

All wardrobe assistants should be able to comprehend impatient instructions delivered in a Xanax haze, and have extensive knowledge of wash-and-wear upholstery fabrics. More important, you have a boldness of spirit that isn't afraid to mix dirt brown with turquoise, and an almost magical ability to finesse lines of sight so that the horizon appears closer, allowing objects in periwinkle polyester to seem miraculously smaller. Most of Mrs. Bush's wardrobe assistants come from the high-fashion retail sector, so an encyclopedic knowledge of the aisles at Target, Dress Barn, and Frugal Fannie's is essential.

Formal Occasions

For formal occasions, Mrs. Bush enjoys the type of one-of-a-kind couture that provokes "Did you make it yourself?" inquiries from delighted dignitaries. When attending state dinners for royalty, she prefers McCall's patterns, which work equally well with denim or corduroy and can be finished off with a comfy pair of pleather slides.

I want to dress like that Katharine Hepburn woman before she died—only with none of those itchy natural fibers. You know, be able to wear slacks all the time without more than a handful of gossipy homos chattering about me looking like Ellen DeGeneres in a cheap Korean wig.

For functions with ambassadors or friendly dictators, a new outfit is not required. Instead, simply retrieve her cabbage-colored pantsuit (the one without the elastic waistband) from the laundry hamper, drench it with "Meadow Rain" Febreze® until there is no trace of Parliament Menthol aroma, and hang it in the shower until many of the creases are no longer discernible from ten feet. Then, fetch her "dress" Dr. Scholl's with the massaging gel insoles (NOTE: These are usually found embedded in the wall just behind the last spot where the President was "eating pretzels" when Mrs. Bush retired for the evening).

The First Lady's Spiritual Assistant

Unlike the California-crazy Nancy Reagan and her astrological charts and Adolfo voodoo dolls, Mrs. Bush simply detests foolish superstitions. Instead, she begins each morning, promptly at 10:20, by invoking the Holy Ghost from His invisible realm to lay waste to her enemies and all who dare to oppose her husband's foreign policy (or hide her cigarettes).

If you are a spiritual assistant to the First Lady, your job includes retrieving, by ten each morning, her "Dog Doo List" and placing it on her Colonial Williamsburg prayer hutch, next to her Franklin Mint "Diana, the People's Princess" doll. After the First Lady has finished reviewing the list of targets for the Lord's wrath, her secretary will then take responsibility for following Mrs. Bush around the building, augmenting and striking names from the list to reflect each murmured exaltation or expletive.[6]

[6] If you hear your name being used by your employer in this dramatic ritual as a result of some minor contretemps during the previous day, do not worry, as Mrs. Bush has only been documented to cause the actual death of one person, and that was a long time ago.

Promptly at 5:00 P.M., Mrs. Bush herself will post the updated Dog Doo List on the metal door of the Sub-Zero with one of her many prized Aunt Jemima refrigerator magnets. When retrieving the list the next morning, you must make sure that the President has not used a marker or condiment to obliterate his own name, as Mrs. Bush will not be fooled by this sneaky redaction. Instead, she will become furious when she reaches the end of her list and cannot utter the ritual closing of "Bad Bushie. Bad, bad Bushie. No bushie for Bushie tonight!"

Medication

If you are one of the First Lady's fleet of personal pharmacists, it is your duty to coordinate with the other licensed ASHP pharmacists to ensure that someone is on call 24/7/365 with keys to the Schedule III cabinets along the corridors on both floors. You are also expected to ensure that the East Wing Self-Serve Pharmacy is well stocked at all times. Other than the patience to assist in prolonged crisis stabilization, your only pertinent job requirement is that you not be color blind, as the First Lady insists that her buffet of daily tablets be arranged in strict accordance with the following pill-consumption protocols: "Blue dolls are washed down with a clear adult beverage; red dolls are taken with a mossy, pleasantly pigmented adult libation."

Wet Bar Safety Concerns

There are thirty-seven "official" wet bars located throughout the White House, not including those appearing on floor plans or in the private residence. They are all double-locked with Schlage dead bolts and retinal or rectal scan, optical-security devices. Only the First Lady has the necessary keys, eyes, and other physical attributes that will allow entry. Be aware that to the right of the glass door of each wet bar, located under an "In Case of Emergency" sign, is a twenty-seven-inch pickax. Please be careful when the twins are visiting or when Mrs. Bush is not on speaking terms with the President. During these times, you will often encounter broken glass and discarded axes in the corridors. It is, therefore, not advised that you traverse the White House in the dark or in stockinged feet.

TOUR GROUPS

~~In keeping with long-standing, unfortunate tradition, members of the general public are permitted to tour White House Inc., which is technically a piece of our wildly bloated National Park System. These tours are free and take place Tuesday through Saturday from 10 A.M. until noon.~~

~~Tickets, which are available on a first-come, first-serve basis, are only required during peak tourism season, which runs from late March through Labor Day. Advance tickets are not available.~~

~~Tours are self-guided and typically take from fifteen to twenty minutes once inside. A brochure is provided that guides visitors through the complex at their own pace.~~

~~Areas open to the public include the Library, former Vermeil room, and the Green, Blue, Red, East, and State Dining rooms. With the exception of security personnel, all employees are directed to avoid these areas during tour hours, lest you suffer the indignity of close proximity to the great unwash~~

> *Praise the Lord on High that we were able to use that terrorist nonsense to keep those damned tourists and their filthy flip-flops and greasy fingers away from the draperies and inlaid floors. I was getting mighty tired of having to slip on my pink Playtex gloves and follow each pack of nobody Japs and wide-eyed Nebraskites with a bucket of barely diluted Lysol. I mean to say, I would have made a few pipe bombs myself if I'd known how quickly it would have gotten rid of those tour groups and—especially—those tacky velvet ropes downstairs. I can't tell you the number of times I told Security that having to limbo under those gosh-darned things in the dark with a full pitcher of margaritas and a lit cigarette was just an accident waiting to happen again!*

Update: Due to heightened security required during the War Against Terrorism, all public tours of the White House have been severely restricted—hopefully permanently. Private, after-hours Congressional Buddy and Ranger-Level Donor tours will, of course, continue as scheduled.

ATTENDING TO THE FIRST TWINS

The First Couple adore their daughters, Jenna and the other one, with the uncritical affection of any parents speaking to reporters inquiring about the children they brought into the world—regardless of how they actually turned out. Indeed, Mr. and Mrs. Bush are so dedicated to maintaining the excitement they feel at the prospect of spending time with Jenna and her darker-haired sister, they diligently try not to risk diminishing the novelty of their daughters' company. This loving goal is achieved by ensuring that family moments not occur with the regularity or duration that imperils the value of all precious things.

As such, the First Twins' parents are often unaware that their daughters are even home. Occasionally they cross paths at the cigarette or Utz snack machines, but that's about it. Nevertheless, life goes on, and inasmuch as housekeeping procedures strictly prohibit vomit-stained carpets, the joy of attending to the First Twins' many needs falls squarely on the shoulders of the White House staff.

The First Twins are like Madagascar aye-ayes; they are strictly nocturnal creatures. They sleep from 6:30 A.M. until approximately 8:15 P.M. each day. Fortunately, this requires no special sound-dampening protocols during normal work hours. Indeed, Security has expressed concern that a Delta Shuttle 737 dropping into the East Wing in the middle of the afternoon would fail to rouse the snoring little darlings from their Corona-drenched slumbers.

Cleanup

If you see orange plastic cones or signs in any of the White House corridors embossed with "Caution: Wet Floor" (and sporting a similar warning in Mexican for the help), chances are the twins are visiting and have returned from a spirited night on the town. If you find Jenna or the other one in a public area and are a housekeeper, use the clean strands of hair to raise the head (don't worry—she won't wake up) and scrub and disinfect the floor surrounding her before gently returning her head to the now-clean flooring. Make sure a cautionary cone is left on either side of the girl, but do not—under any circumstance—attempt to awaken a First Twin without protective eyewear.

Parents need to instill plenty of self-esteem in their children so they don't wind up working in a library somewhere and marry the first alcoholic that comes along and slurs the question!

Food Preparation

When it comes to solid nutrition, both of the Bush children live almost exclusively on bowls of mixed nuts, Pepperidge Farm Goldfish and hot-chicken wings. As far as the kitchen staff can ascertain, it appears that the girls frequent places that provide for this regimented diet, as they have yet to eat anything other than chewing gum in the White House.

A "Woof Woof" Welcome from Spotty & Barney

Hi there! We are the First Doggies. Our names are Barney and Spotty. Our daddy and mommy are President and Mrs. Bush. We're allowed to go anywhere in the White House, so you will get to meet us soon! We are mostly friendly, so do not be afraid to pet us—even if we growl, snap, or bare our professionally capped teeth.

Our daddy and mommy love us very much—even more than those two girls who stole our neutering painkillers and tried to make us lick honey off them. Mommy and Daddy only like employees whom they see always being extra-nice to us and never rudely shoving us away when be burrow our drippy snouts deep into their crotches. You would do well to remember that.

We like yummy bones, deep paw massages, gourmet doggie chocolates, and squeaky Tom Daschle chew toys. But more than anything, we love to give kisses. We especially like to kiss faces. Faces are salty, and we like the taste of salt after tongue-grooming our hole hair. Sometimes we can kiss one face for forty-five whole minutes!

Welcome to White House Inc. We can't wait to be your bestest friends!

Love,

Spotty

Barney

CARING FOR THE FIRST PETS

 As the First Lady is fond of saying, "I love Jenna and my other daughter, but I actually *enjoy* the company of my little pets." As such, the staff is seldom called upon to tend the needs of the First Pets. There are, however, times when the First Lady is unable to get about with sufficient haste to effectively intercede during her pets' frequent evacuations of waste or to otherwise tend to their freely expressed demands. It is, therefore, necessary for all staff, including cabinet members, to become familiar with the exacting requirements of the First Pets.

First Pet Food Preparation

When the First Lady's "boys" are good, which is always, they are entitled to their favorite treat: handmade leather footwear. If one of the First Pets has designated part of your shoe for partial digestion, it is ill advised that you not churlishly attempt to remove your Ferragamo from the pet's jaw unless you crave a septic ankle.

If during the course of the day, the First Pets do not become sated with sufficient cowhide, they will wander into the State Dining Room and howl for service. If a diplomatic dinner is in progress, the resourceful pets will leap from table to table, availing themselves of whatever food has been served until the White House chef is summoned so that they may yelp à la carte selections.

Canine Couture

During the blustery Washington winter, the First Lady's pets are to be dressed each morning with one of their many monogrammed Isle of Skye Scottish cashmere sweaters, tail warmers, and booties. DO NOT mix a savannah-colored sweater with a camel-colored accessory (or vice versa) as this will enrage the First Lady and make the First Pets unwilling to go outside. In warmer months, a Victorian toile jean jacket over a petite Ralph Lauren cotton shirt with a Peter Pan collar is appropriate for everyday, nonformal functions. No dog is to leave its New Zealand sheepskin-covered mahogany sleigh bed without a delightful spritzing of its preferred Angus Weare eau de parfum. All dogs (as well as the First Twins) are to be outfitted with their tailored snood (in the plaid suitable to their clan) before drinking any liquids to avoid the unsightliness of wet ears (or, in the case of the First Twins, split ends covered in coarse salt).

X.
SERVING AT THE PLEASURE OF THE PRESIDENT

MISCONDUCT

In order to facilitate management of potential scandals that could arise from incidents of personnel misconduct, White House Inc. has established an internal Office to Oversee Potential Scandals (OOPS). Comprised of representatives from Corporate Security, Risk Management, and the Department of Faith, the office also maintains a small rotating staff of CIA debriefing specialists and is responsible for educating employees on acceptable conduct—whether in the office, at home, abroad, or even on a broad.

OOPS accomplishes its mission in part through the printing and dissemination of "The White House Way," a breezy, fun, 800-page pamphlet covering a handful of key misconduct-specific rules and regulations—along with associated fines, penalties, and demerits for each. "The White House Way" is required reading and must be purchased at the employee store ($249.99) within seven days of your hiring. Failure to do so is punishable in the intensely unpleasant manner that is briefly outlined somewhere deep within the 137 chapters of "The White House Way."

In the extremely brief interim period before you acquire your copy, you may peruse the following important excerpt from "The White House Way":

The Five Deadly Sins of White House Conduct

As an employee of White House Inc., it is expected that you will be on your best behavior at all times. You are representing the Republican Party, the President of the United States, Jesus Christ, and a long list of well-groomed, top-brass corporate donors whose lips purse easily. As such, you must avoid the Five Deadly Sins of White House Conduct at all costs, lest your respect for the traditions and ideologies we hold dear ever be called into question.

Mercy: Acts of mercy are for ignorant, misguided liberals who steal votes by giving away free meals and cigarettes to minorities who will do anything for a free van ride to a heated elementary-school gymnasium. We don't cater to such bleeding-heart nonsense here. If you are looking for a break or a freebie, or if you conduct yourself in a manner that suggests you are a mercy addict (inclined to pity or possess feelings for those who are divinely saddled with misfortune), you are likely to quickly join the legions of unemployed so that you may even more fully empathize with their wretched plight.

"Mercy" is just a word our maid Beulah squeals when she drops a plate in the kitchen!

🚫 **Charity:** If you are giving something away, you should always expect something tangible back in return, whether an IRS-recognized deduction or the gratitude of someone in a position to help you. The problem with the more traditional concepts of charity is that you don't get anything back that you can amortize. Yes, you sometimes enjoy a tingly sensation in your nether regions purely for being more generous than people who have nothing, but that doesn't last long enough to actually be worth squat.

As a White House Inc. staffer, it is completely unacceptable for you to be involved in anything that could even remotely implicate you or your employer in acts that might result in some lazy nobody collecting a handout. If you should find yourself trapped in a scenario when being a party to charity is unavoidable, make every effort to leverage the unpleasantness of the occasion with a hastily prepared press release or (if the colored recipients look pitiful enough) a photo opportunity. Such enterprising publicizing of would-be selflessness can, if packaged correctly, engender public awareness of simulated nobility within White House Inc.'s ranks.

🚫 **Social Responsibility:** In the words of Jesus Christ, "For the poor always ye have with you"—John 12:8. In the words of your CEO, "Never question what the Lord Jesus says." That's why, whether He's affirmatively axing education grants, eviscerating social programs that feed poor babies, or vociferously rejecting exit-ramp squeegee services, President Bush does everything in His power to preserve the Lord's carefully designed caste system of dissolute misery. Fortunately, no White House Inc. employee would ever dare flaunt such hubris as to tinker with the Lord's righteous allocations of blessings!

🚫 **Accountability:** Your President, like all functioning nondyslexics, is not a big fan of tongue-tripping words with more than one syllable. Even the paradoxical "monosyllabic" perversely taunts from the teleprompter. So, naturally, "accountability" has yet to make its fancy-pants way into his lexicon. Nevertheless, when the going gets tough, the President is not so partisan as to abstain from invoking Democratic President Harry S. Truman's cry of "The buck stops here!" On these fabulously rare occasions, pay close attention at whom He is pointing when repeating this historic phrase, so that you will know which office will soon be available.

🚫 **Reading Banned Books:** The aftermath of September 11 has led to a great spiritual reawakening in America. Among the signs of the Holy Spirit are the glorious bonfires He is lighting in church parking lots all across America. These righteous infernos glow with a hungry rage for Michael Moore, Harry Potter, Hillary Clinton, and other flammable offenses to God-fearing Americans. Book burnings are wonderful community events, and the whole family can get involved. Republican children find that choosing a book is often as much fun as watching its pages blacken and curl just before the binding ignites in glorious testament to the fiery destiny that awaits all who sin.

GRIEVANCES

White House Inc. is committed to handling employee complaints in the most effective way possible: preventing you from making them. As such, various procedures have been established to ensure the fair and balanced prior resolution of all grievances.

☆ **NOTE: Should you decide it is necessary to reveal your pathological inability to be happy in even the most amenable of work environments, you may submit your grievance to senior management via the suggestion box (see p. 194). Please remember, though, that while your complaint is being dispatched, at no time may you disturb other workers with the trivial details of whatever alleged fault you may be imagining.**

Grievance Preclusion Strategies

1. **Harmony Development Seminar:** All employees are preregistered for this all-day seminar, which is taught on the second day of orientation by senior representatives from Corporate Security. Part lecture and part interactive, the seminar includes a PowerPoint presentation, an informative virtual tour of the corporate detention center, and a vomit-inducing snuff film of untraceable origin. Upon completion of the course, you will be awarded a handsome "Happy Camper" certificate that you may hang in your cubicle. White House Inc. finds this class is the most effective way of disabusing newcomers of the potentially harmful notions that lead the reckless to second-guess their superiors.

2. **Prescription-Strength Contentment:** More often than not, the sensation of intense anxiety that precedes the filing of unfounded grievances is the product of a physiological imbalance. Should you find yourself inexplicably dwelling on critical or otherwise illicit thoughts, it's probably time to visit the White House physician for a mental examination. He can diagnose your condition and select an appropriate pharmaceutical cocktail within a matter of minutes. Please follow the instructions on the foil sample packs carefully. Fortunately, since the majority of the drugs prescribed here at White House Inc. are highly habit-forming, you should experience little difficulty remembering to take them. Your initial hundred-pill supply is free, but after that, the full brand-name prescription price will be deducted from your paycheck. And while this may seem costly at times, you will find that it's better to sacrifice an extra few thousand dollars per month than to endure painful and gossip-inducing withdrawal. After all, it's hard to successfully conduct a press conference when you're flopping around in the corridors like a dockside tuna.

3. **Prefrontal Fulfillment:** Occasionally, employees may find that they are unresponsive to chemical grievance-prevention treatment. Such individuals may suffer from an array of unpleasant symptoms, including the perception of discrimination, scrutinizing what they are told, or an irrepressible desire to visit the suggestion box. If this describes you, the recommended course of action is to have the troublesome part of your abnormal brain frappéd with a scalpel whisk before it causes you to voluntarily eject yourself from the building and be hounded by poisonous references that ruin your career. Your health-insurance plan does not cover this procedure, but Human Resources will be happy to recommend a good conservative neurosurgeon specializing in the removal of wayward synapses that compel the undisciplined mind to dangerously question input.

THE SUGGESTION BOX

Directly abutting the rear of the furnace in the Garbage Incinerator Room, you'll find a weathered, wooden suggestion box. Using the blank golf scorecards and stubby wooden pencils provided, please feel free to scribble down any opinions or suggestions you may have. When finished, drop positive comments through the top slot marked "Team Player Feedback" and any negative comments or grievances into the lower slot marked "Other." In the likely event this latter slot is glowing red and/or smoldering, please exercise caution to not suffer any burns of a severity that might decrease your productivity.

(i) **It is a long-standing White House Inc. tradition for elder employees to pen incriminating, often bawdy, suggestions in the name of new employees. Unluckily for you, in today's post-9/11 climate, the National Security Advisor has demanded that Human Resources treat even the most laughable forgeries as if they are genuinely serious. Therefore, do not be alarmed in the likely event that management moves to implement "your" idea to begin stockpiling a painful array of office supplies inside your "cavernous" rectum. Note also that finding slips of notepaper reading "FAGGOT" taped to your back is another reliable indication that someone has been peppering the suggestion box with misattributed comments. These zany corporate high jinks are all in good fun—and serve as a wonderful test of your ability to blend in.**

DISCIPLINARY ACTION

We pride ourselves here at White House Inc. in being frank. So when it comes to disciplinary action, we will simply say that how important you are will dictate the likelihood and severity of discipline. For example, if five people report to you, they each share a 20 percent chance that they will be disciplined for your mistakes, crimes, and errors in taste or judgment. If you report directly to the President, punishment for misconduct might be handed to you in the form of a first-class plane ticket, the password to a Swiss bank account, and a few suitcases you will need to pack for a redemptive Caribbean vacation that will keep you out of the public eye until you are ready for your appointment to President Jeb Bush's cabinet. If you are one of the fungible drones who toil to make someone who matters looks good, your discipline will involve signing a voluminous confession of isolated personal moral turpitude, after which you will be sacrificed to the criminal justice system and/or given a short-lived show on MSNBC.

TERMINATION

As a bona fide federal bureaucrat, you need never suffer the bourgeois humiliation of being formally terminated. Should you, however, reach a point in your White House Inc. career when your continued presence is determined to be politically injurious to the corporation, you will be tasked with composing a press release claiming you are departing voluntarily to spend more time with your family. Management will dictate how the departure will be characterized through our own channels in the media.

Should you arrive at work one morning to find the cube mate you "thought you knew" has a different face, or is taller or shorter than you remembered him to be, you would be correct in assuming that the person who was sitting next to you on the previous day has voluntarily terminated himself. Take comfort in the knowledge that this corporation is so efficient, it can effortlessly replace any one of its subservient data-mining cogs within any given twenty-four-hour period. Of course, this is something you might wish to bear in mind should you ever start to feel unnecessarily important.

RESIGNATION

If you read the newspapers, you may be working under the misapprehension that people voluntarily resign from White House Inc. The uninformed who embrace such wistful conceits tend to also assume that members of the Costa Nostra are free to make career changes. So that we are clear: You are working at President Bush's pleasure and convenience, not your own. As such, you will leave when He says so and under the cloud He confects to suit the spin to be attached to your departure.

For those of you who contemplate terminating your employment before White House Inc. has completely wrung you dry, you may find it helpful to contemplate whether you and your family are so immune to the disgusted taunts of others that you can withstand a lifetime of character assassination through a relentless stream of well-placed but untraceable leaks.

After such careful consideration, if you are still prepared to venture out onto the treacherous path of living your so-called own life, notify Human Resources no less than thirteen (13) months prior to your intended date of departure. During this time, the Vice President's office will cordially interrogate you and establish a plausible deniability file for any sensitive matters you may have been exposed to, as well as proactively prepare assertions of immunity to assist in the stonewalling of any congressional subpoenas concerning your role here at White House Inc. When asked, you are to sign the stack of blank affidavits presented to you.

During your final weeks at White House Inc., you will undergo several dozen sessions of medium-voltage electroshock therapy. This regrettable but necessary exit-interview procedure will result in your suits clinging to your legs in an unsightly fashion and undermine your ability to provide credible testimony in any future inquiry. Prior to submitting to this final step in your release from employment, we suggest that you begin sticking a few Post-its on your desk to remind you where you put your car keys, whether you are married, and if you have any children.

XI.
ACKNOWLEDGMENT OF RECEIPT AND UNDERSTANDING

ACKNOWLEDGMENT OF RECEIPT AND UNDERSTANDING

I, the undersigned White House Inc. employee, have read and committed to memory the *White House Inc. Employee Handbook*. I hereby pledge to maintain its contents in the strictest confidence for the duration of my days here on Earth. Should I fail to do so, whether by leaking to a journalist, Democrat, or otherwise detestable, misbegotten creation of the Lord, I hereby indemnify and hold harmless White House Inc. for any and all costs of denial in the likely event that my bloated corpse is found in a remote landfill clutching a government-issue suicide note.

Signed,

Name: _____

Date: _____

ADDITIONAL READING

THE WHITE HOUSE
WWW.WHITEHOUSE.ORG

WHITEHOUSE.ORG is the officious website of George W. Bush, the 43rd President of the United States. In an era when the levers of mass media power are jealously guarded by America-despising liberals, our Christ-appointed leader has commandeered Al Gore's World Wide Interweb as a convenient (albeit nerdy) channel through which to deliver his gospel directly to the legions of affluent white folks who came within spitting distance of legitimately electing him. Only on WHITEHOUSE.ORG can you enjoy the very latest news on President Bush's Administration, policy initiatives, and inspired strategy to protect America from global adulation. You'll also find extensive inside information on the First Lady, the U.S. Department of Faith, a super-fun "For Kids Only!" section, and an exciting Gift Shop filled to the digital rafters with all manner of patriotism-affirming fashions, posters, and fiendishly covetable bric-a-brac. God Bless America!

LANDOVER BAPTIST CHURCH
WWW.LANDOVERBAPTIST.ORG

"Where the Worthwhile Worship. Unsaved Unwelcome."

The President's chosen place of worship sits on 7,000 acres of Godly Iowa countryside. Boasting over 58,000 members, 2,000 salaried staffers, 7 Gated Christian Communities, 2 PGA "Church Members Only" Golf Courses, several Christian Malls, 14 Chapels, the world-famous "Blood of the Lamb" Christian steakhouse, a Baptist police force, 21 assisted-living centers, four Christian schools, a Baptist University, The Center for Creation Science Research, the Giant Demon Skeletons Museum, two hospitals, a Christian lake, retreat centers, spas, and a talking parrot that wins souls—the Landover Baptist Church is the largest assembly of True Christians™, on Earth. If you are Truly Saved™, you are welcome to visit our church website. If you are "unsaved," please do not bother us, for we are about the Lord's business. Glory!

Mrs Betty Bowers
america's best christian
WWW.BETTYBOWERS.COM

Unchic? Unsaved? Wavering faith? Wandering hands? A pair of $800 Jimmy Choos that won't work with your Laura Bush polyblend pantsuit? Simply ask yourself, as all Republican cognoscenti in a pickle have learned to do: "What Would Betty Do?"

Mrs. Betty Bowers, America's most puritanical pundit, is so close to Jesus, He uses her birthday when He buys Lotto tickets. She even has His economical loaves and fish recipe. Of all of this country's neocon zealots, only Mrs. Bowers knows how many shopping days there are until the Apocalypse—and which sins the Lord is most forgetful about, allowing her to slip through the "Ten Sins or Less" express line come Judgment Day. As Betty is fond of saying when convivial conversation wanes at White House dinners: "If God created me in His image, I have more than returned the compliment."